D0950104

Stick it to The Man

Stick it to The Man

How to Skirt the Law, Scam Your
Enemies, and Screw Big, Fat, Stupid,
Lazy Corporations . . . For Fun and Profit!

Ronald Lewis

Skyhorse Publishing

Skyhorse Publishing books may be purchased in bulk at special discounts for sales promotion, corporate gifts, fund-raising, or educational purposes. Special editions can also be created to specifications. For details, contact the Special Sales Department, Skyhorse Publishing, 555 Eighth Avenue, Suite 903, New York, NY 10018 or info@skyhorsepublishing.com.

www.skyhorsepublishing.com

10 9 8 7 6 5 4 3 2 1

Library of Congress Cataloging-in-Publication Data
Lewis, Ronald.
  Stick it to the man : How to skirt the law, scam your enemies, and screw big, fat, stupid, lazy corporations . . . for fun and profit! / Ronald Lewis.
      p. cm.
  ISBN 978-1-60239-641-8
 1. Consumer satisfaction. 2. Fraud. 3. Swindlers and swindling. I. Title.
  HF5415.335.L48 2009
  381.3'4—dc22
                        2009000235

Printed in China

For my mom, Helen, whose love and guidance is priceless to me.

In life, we are often led through darkness without any sign of light. Those who seek it are best prepared to break the spell which rules the subconscious mind. Breaking free of the grip of man is the most priceless act of humanity.

CONTENTS

Introduction   xvii

Twenty-Four Self-Employment Ideas to Avoid
  Modern-Day Slavery A.K.A. a Job   1

The Coffee Shop and You: Getting the Best Bang
  for the Cup   5

Your Cell-Phone Carrier and You (Part One):
  Standing Up to the Tyranny of "Contract Tricks"   7

Your Cell-Phone Carrier and You (Part Two):
  Changing Your Mind about a New Phone   10

Your Cell-Phone Carrier and You (Part Three):
  Protecting Your Investment without
  Breaking the Bank   12

Your Cell-Phone Carrier and You (Part Four):
  Replacing the Brick   14

Your Cell-Phone Carrier and You (Part Five):
  They Say You're a "Motor Mouth"   16

Your Cell-Phone Carrier and You (Part Six):
  Dealing with Carriers Other than Ma Bell   19

Your Cell-Phone Carrier and You (Part Seven):
  Escaping the Bondage of "Contract Hell"   21

Creative Tactics to Attract Publicity
  (without a PR Agency)   23

The Walled Garden of Apple (Part One):
  iPod and iTunes   27

The Walled Garden of Apple (Part Two):
Downloading Movies Beyond iTunes   29

The Walled Garden of Apple (Part Three):
Protecting Your Music Collection   30

Oh, Canada: Extending Your Stay without
Documentation or Hassle   32

Big-Box Retailers and You: Getting a
Better Deal You Can Live With   35

Computer Software and You:
Finding Alternatives to Microsoft   37

Good-bye Microsoft and Apple:
Hello Linux and Netbooks   39

Ditching Your Computer Company
After the Purchase   41

Getting Rid of the Garbage on
Your New Computer: A Primer on "Crapware"   43

The Federal Reserve: Forcing the
World's Most Secretive Crooks into a Corner
(and Taking Back What's Yours)   45

The Power of Free Software (Part One):
How One Man Reinvented the Telephone
and the Way We Communicate   50

The Power of Free Software (Part Two):
How Google Built a Multibillion-Dollar Empire   54

Throwing Out the Company Behind
Your Computer Warranty   56

Keeping the Printer Company Off Your Back
   and In Check   58

"Winning a Round of Boxing"
   with the Big-Box Retailers   61

Dealing with Big-Box Retailers' Secret Web Sites   63

Dealing with Retail Outlets that Demand You
   Show Your Receipt at the Door   65

Waking Up from *The Matrix* and
   Stickin' It to Retailers on "Black Friday"   67

Demanding Better Service from Companies with
   Horrible Phone Support   72

The Unprofessional Truck Driver and You:
   Don't Be Bullied   74

Running Circles around Companies that Won't Let
   You Cancel Your Service   76

Addressing Companies with
   Crappy Customer Service   79

Socking It to Companies that Require
   You Sign a "Mandatory Binding Arbitration"
   Clause (Part One)   82

Socking It to Companies that Require
   You Sign a "Mandatory Binding Arbitration"
   Clause (Part Two)   85

Socking It to Companies that Require
   You Sign a "Mandatory Binding Arbitration"
   Clause (Part Three)   87

No More Cold, Crappy Fast Food:
Have it Fresh, Hot, and Now!   88

Standing Toe-to-Toe with
Your Local Hospital (Part One)   90

Standing Toe-to-Toe with
Your Local Hospital (Part Two)   96

Insuring Yourself against the Shady Practices of
Insurance Companies   98

Staying a Step Ahead of Your Airline (Part One)   103

Staying a Step Ahead of Your Airline (Part Two)   107

Wringing Out the Benefits of Your Airline's
Frequent-Flier-Miles Program   109

An Informed Flier Is a Happy Flier: Being More
Cleaver than Your Fellow Airline Passengers   112

Finding a Deal at a Hotel (Part One)   113

Finding a Deal at a Hotel (Part Two)   115

Avoiding the Pitfalls of Travel Web Sites   117

Skip the Local Car Mechanic: Be Your Own for
Pennies on the Dollar   119

Negotiating Your Way to a
Better Deal at the Gym   120

Living for Free at a Mall's Expense   123

College Textbooks: Learning Well on a
"Ramen Noodles Budget"   124

Greedy Banks and Creative Ways to Bank an
Outcome in Your Favor (Part One)   126

Greedy Banks and Creative Ways to Bank an
  Outcome in Your Favor (Part Two)   129

Greedy Banks and Creative Ways to Bank an
  Outcome in Your Favor (Part Three)   131

Showing Your Credit-Card Company How Much
  You Love Them (Part One)   132

Showing Your Credit-Card Company How Much
  You Love Them (Part Two)   137

Busting the Chops of Telemarketers   139

Game Over for the Most Annoying "Pitchmen"
  on the Internet: Spammers   143

The Money Bandits: Protecting Yourself from
  Credit Card and Identity Thieves   145

The Art of Law and Sticking It to Those
  Who Stick It to Others   146

Finding an Honest, Hardworking Realtor
  (Who Will Work for You)   147

"Shock and Awe" Your Way around the
  Local Car Dealer (Part One)   149

"Shock and Awe" Your Way around the
  Local Car Dealer (Part Two)   151

"Shock and Awe" Your Way around the
  Local Car Dealer (Part Three)   155

Beating the Parking Ticket (and the Meter Maid)   158

Outsmarting the Cop Waiting to
  Catch You Speeding   161

Getting Down to Business with the IRS
  (and Having a "One-Up," Too)   163

Throwing 'em Overboard: Shareholders
  Fight Back against a "Mega Corporation"
  and Its Stupid Executives   167

"Trimming the Fat" from Your Rent   171

The Right Way to Address Your Rude,
  Loud, Sloppy Neighbors   173

"Throwing a Shoe" at Your Local Tax Collector   174

"Serving the Pork" to Your Congressperson   176

The Cartel Known as OPEC   178

Being Smarter than Your Boss
  (While Smiling Your Way to the Bank)   180

Acknowledgments   183

INTRODUCTION

Hello and welcome to *Stick It To The Man*. I am pleased that you chose to add this book to your collection. I am incredibly grateful that you did. *Stick It* was a labor of love, to say the least. The ideas, examples, and stories included here are broad, clever, unique, and even controversial. There's truly something for everyone that can be applied to everyday life and experiences.

We (publisher, editors, mentors, and I) attempted to strike a balance between light-hearted advice and effective, practical tips. I believe you'll find many entertaining moments in this book, as well as a great opportunity to feed your mind with new and interesting information. Here's just a sampling of things to expect in the pages to follow:

- Playing hardball with hospitals to save thousands on health care
- Giving a "black eye" to retailers on "Black Friday"
- "Respectfully frustrating" a truck driver for being aggressive on the road
- Dealing with obnoxious, crazy, and disrespectful neighbors
- Trumping your boss in the workplace—the boss you'd love to choke and shove in a closet

If you can, take a few pictures of "The Man" holding a copy of *Stick It* and send them to me. Most of all, do everything with a smile, and make sure to high-five your mates along the way!

We hope you'll enjoy this book and share it with your friends, family, and coworkers. We think everyone will get a serious kick out of this book because anyone can relate to the scenarios presented within. You are also encouraged to share your stories and experiences on my Web site as well.

Make it STICK—and good,

RONALD L. LEWIS II

Stick It Commander-In-Chief

www.ronaldlewis.com/stickittotheman

www.ronaldlewis.com

Stick it to The Man

TWENTY-FOUR SELF-EMPLOYMENT IDEAS TO AVOID MODERN-DAY SLAVERY A.K.A. A JOB

There's no greater freedom in life than turning in a two-week notice to your manager. It is the beginning of ending ridiculous work hours, missing precious time with family and friends, and a paltry allotment of vacation time. Whether you're a seasoned serial entrepreneur who returned to the workforce or someone who's dreaming of being in control of his or her own destiny, self-employment is and always will be the ticket to real freedom.

World-renowned motivational speaker Les Brown had this to say at one of his seminars about jobs and layoffs: "When I hear about layoffs, I don't see people losing their jobs—I see people who have an opportunity."

For those who don't have major commitments, such as children, a mortgage, or spouse, you are encouraged to break the rules and go for broke. We live in a world today where no job is guaranteed, no matter how many degrees or talents one might have. If you're still stuck in a job, no matter how great it is or how much it pays, you should still be thinking beyond the cube about what you can contribute to society with the power of your mind.

I will not tell you that self-employment is perfect because it is not. I will not tell you that it's paradise. I will not tell you that it's the quickest path to riches. Self-employment is about creativity, imagination, ingenuity, and dedication. It could take you months—or years—to hit your stride. There are many variables and unknowns in the self-employment world, but they shouldn't prevent you from trying new ideas and challenging yourself to do more independently of a job.

The most important thing to know is this: You will fail. Don't be discouraged by failure. In fact, embrace it with a fierce force, because it's the only way you will learn and improve your success over time. Failure is our ultimate lesson in life. Do not wallow in self-pity or depression. Pick yourself up, brush off the dirt, and start thinking about where things went wrong so that you can avoid similar pitfalls in the future.

Ready to dip your toes into the pool of possibilities? Here are 24 ideas to jumpstart your journey.

CULPRIT: The cubicle

PROBLEM: It's a dead-end.

WAYS TO FREE YOURSELF AND SOAR:

- Start a podcast or blog in your area of expertise
- Become a freelance writer for major blogs and media outlets
- Launch a unique airport courier service for high-net-worth individuals (offer wireless Internet, bottle service, dry cleaning, etc.)
- Become an independent talent scout and discover the next hot band

- Write whitepapers for major companies
- Become a virtual assistant to small-business owners
- Manage the lives of wealthy families (vacations, errands, etc.)
- Become an independent property manager
- Start a catering business which exclusively serves CEOs and celebrities around the world
- Become a fashion consultant to teens and individuals with disposable income
- Start an interior decorating business which caters to newlyweds
- Launch a "green" consulting business that works with communities to develop effective recycling programs
- Start an "airline liaison" consultancy to assist airline employees (pilots and flight attendants) with matters they're unable to address while traveling
- Prepare tasty meals for busy families with a household income of at least $250,000
- Become a "makeover consultant" to new jobseekers
- Design business cards and brochures for new businesses
- Run errands for wealthy elderly couples (someone will gladly pay for the convenience)
- Start a trash collection service for rural communities
- Deliver gourmet meals in style to business meetings
- Investigate ways of creating "residual income" with new, innovative concepts

- Start an Internet-based phone company which caters to small businesses (See "The Power of Free Software (Part One)" for an idea)
- Record business meetings (audio and video) and provide CDs and MP3s to attendees for future reference
- Become a "hospitality evangelist" for cities or states
- Become a tour guide for convention attendees

So, there you have it—twenty-four ideas to inspire you to attain office freedom. Go get 'em, tiger!

THE COFFEE SHOP AND YOU: GETTING THE BEST BANG FOR THE CUP!

Let's face it, human beings are addicted to coffee. Whether it's because we're fascinated by the fact that we're drinking roasted bean water or captured by the aroma, many of us can't go a day without having our caffeinated fix. Fortunately, the average coffee addict has a plethora of choices: Coffee shops are everywhere! Many are even one-stop shops for hot drinks, sandwiches, and treats. Their environment is usually friendly, comforting, and cheery.

Unfortunately, not all "coffee fix" runs are pleasant. Some are a pure nightmare. Imagine tasting the bitterest coffee you've ever had, or someone sneezing over your cup of joe. Worse, how about someone adding their own flavoring to the mix with their own saliva? So, how does one get the best bang for the cup? Let's find out!

CULPRIT: Your favorite coffee shop

PROBLEM: Bad, makes-your-skin-crawl coffee!

THE PAYBACK DREAMS ARE MADE OF: Here's one prank a group of people pulled off in San Francisco:

They selected several coffee shops belonging to a well-known corporation.

They jammed the locks and posted Closed and For Lease signs on as many as seventeen of their San Francisco–area stores in the middle of the night.

These same signs also announced that thousands of their retail locations worldwide were being closed.

The signs also announced that the company was closing these stores to "make room for local coffee bars."

THE SENSIBLE APPROACH: To avoid being hauled off to jail (without a lifeline to save your bacon), here are a few things to consider if your coffee-shop experience is anything but great:

- Talk to the manager about the inconsistency of your coffee experience.
- Politely ask and wait for a new cup of coffee.
- Return your coffee and politely ask for a refund.
- Write a review about the coffee shop on Yelp.com, CitySearch, or a similar Web site to alert others about your experience.
- Stop patronizing the location.

All in all, you control the outcome of the experience you expect at your favorite coffee shop.

YOUR CELL-PHONE CARRIER AND YOU (PART ONE): STANDING UP TO THE TYRANNY OF "CONTRACT TRICKS"

Cell phones are as ubiquitous as those beings we call "humans"—you simply cannot avoid either! On any given day, someone's talking on one on the street, in the car, on the bus, or in the stall in the restroom (that has to be really awkward, eh?). Many are literally attached to the hip, stored inside purses and bras, or temporarily displaced under a pile of week-old, funk-infested clothes.

Regardless of where your cell phone is kept, it has revolutionized our world and how we communicate. They've become small, effective devices to keep us in touch with loved ones, our colleagues, bill collectors (for those who answer their phones), psycho exes, and even doorbells!

What's the most unpleasant part of owning a cell phone? You have to play by the rules established by your carrier, which isn't always fun. After all, they own the network and infrastructure, so we must abide by their tricks, terms, and silly contracts, which are filled with a bunch of legal mumbo jumbo (how often do people read those things, anyway?). We may not be tethered by a cord to our carrier; however, they've managed to deploy invisible strings over the air to keep us in check. Where's the freedom in talking again?

Considering the grip your cell-phone company has on you and your life, it's probably one of the companies in your life that frustrates you the most. Fortunately, there are a few ways to loosen the noose and break free of their stranglehold!

CULPRIT: Big, bad, ugly cell-phone company

PROBLEM: Restrictive, soul-choking contracts

THE SMART THING TO DO: Let's say you really want to break free of the "cell jail" (contract), but you don't want to pay the early termination fee (ETF). If this sounds like your situation, here's a way to sock it to 'em and laugh your way to freedom:

꜏ Watch for rate changes by your carrier that would materially affect your plan.

꜏ When a rate change like this occurs, it's your right to cancel your plan. Yes, you read that correctly. Your right. They won't necessarily tell you, but rest assured that you do have the right. Here's a simple way to monitor rate changes:

  ⟋ Visit Google News at news.google.com.

  ⟋ Create a news alert for yourself with these search terms: [carrier name], rate, change.

Meanwhile, if your carrier changes rates on a plan other than your *existing* plan, quickly change your plan to the plan that will have the upcoming change. This will enable you to get out of your contract once the change actually happens.

BONUS! If you check out cell-phone carriers like Credo Mobile, you will find that in an effort to get you to become their customer, they will pay your existing cell company's ETF for you. Not a bad deal!

YOUR CELL-PHONE CARRIER AND YOU (PART TWO): CHANGING YOUR MIND ABOUT A NEW PHONE

It seems that every day, cell-phone manufacturers are releasing newer and better models. Your coworker just picked up an iPhone, while your boss is raving about his new Google Android–based phone. They both have all the whiz-bang features to make you drool for days: GPS, colorful displays, useful applications, and so on.

Immediately, you want something better, because you're not happy with what appears to be something from yesteryear: a basic, cracked, half-working Nokia from a hundred years ago. You want the good stuff, so you make the impulse decision to visit your parole officer (the cell-phone company) about acquiring some new gear. But when you go to your cell-phone company to get one, they tell you:

The price of the phone for *you* is outrageously high because your existing contract is not up yet. ("Bait, shackle, and throw away the key until the day of parole.")

Yes, your contract is expiring soon, so you *can* get that phone at the discounted price . . . but you will have to sign a new two-year contract to get it. ("How dare you ask about a new phone before your parole—here's an extension for thinking you're better than us.")

Sheesh! These guys are difficult, aren't they? Fortunately, there are *always* options!

CULPRIT: Selfish cell-phone company

PROBLEM: Stifling consumer options for a new phone

A FEW IDEAS TO WORK SMARTER AND GET WHAT YOU WANT: If you still want that new phone and you don't want to pay the full price for it and/or you don't want to sign a new two-year contract, just remember this:

You don't have to buy your new phone directly from your cell carrier.

You can get a new phone anywhere you want, so you don't have to pay their inflated prices or sign any kind of contract at all.

And here are some places where you might go to get a new phone:

- eBay
- TigerDirect.com
- Use one of many "cell-phone swapping" sites like Cell-TradeUSA.com to switch phones and/or carriers.

YOUR CELL-PHONE CARRIER AND YOU (PART THREE): PROTECTING YOUR INVESTMENT WITHOUT BREAKING THE BANK

In some cases, the purchase of insurance for your phone is a good thing. If it's a $20 Wal-Mart special, there really isn't a point. However, if you own an iPhone, BlackBerry Storm, or something similar, it might be worthwhile to consider insuring it. Unfortunately, like all things we love to dislike about the cell-phone industry, insurance is a tricky affair, too.

Here's how the system seems to work: the *more* you spend on your phone, the *worse* customer service they offer you. More specifically, when you buy an *el-cheapo* phone, they'll sell you insurance for it for about $5/month. But when you buy an *expensive* phone, what you hear when you ask about insurance is usually, "Nope, sorry, sucker. Now that you fell in love with that expensive beast, you're screwed. We *won't* insure it for you because, well, it's an expensive beast and we don't want to take the risk. So you're on your on, pal. Hey, thanks for the sale . . . and good luck."

Best of all, here's what the sneaky pranksters *won't* tell you: after you drop and break that slippery, expensive beast, it's going to cost you three to five times more to replace it than it cost you to buy it in the first place. The *nerve* of these guys, eh?

In other words: Owning an expensive cell phone *without* insurance is a game that only fools should play. Why be a fool when you can play and win?

CULPRIT: The infamous company that sells you wireless phone service

PROBLEM: Their asinine cell-phone insurance tactics

THE ANSWER TO THE PROBLEM: No matter what kind of phone you have, tell them to grill their insurance and serve it to those willing to accept it. Instead, go to www. SquareTrade.com and buy your cell-phone warranty there, because unlike your crappy cell-phone company, they will sell you a warranty for any kind of phone for less than your carrier sells insurance. (Yes, they'll even insure your iPhone.)

Who says you have to be the cell-phone company's fool?

YOUR CELL-PHONE CARRIER AND YOU (PART FOUR): REPLACING THE BRICK

Don't you just love it when your cell phone stops working? You've tried everything in your power to resurrect it and, after many tries, you've finally given up. Now, whether or not the result of your phone not working is due to a malfunction or abuse (be honest, you dropped it a few times while trying to impress your friends with the "balancing act"), the process of getting it repaired or replaced is nothing short of falling off a building in a bad dream.

Cell-phone companies are not in the business of losing money. They'd rather cut your hands off than provide you with a working phone. How do these guys stay in business again? Oh, right, by dragging you along by the head and giving you what they want. They understand what they can get away with and what you can't. That's right, they suffer from the grand illusion that they have the upper hand (only because people aren't reading this book!), but as you'll figure out (if you haven't already), there are a million options for railroading these guys and getting what you want.

CULPRIT: That pesky, annoying cell-phone company (again!)

PROBLEM: It's hell to get a phone replacement.

SOLUTION: Get the working cell phone you're due. So your cell phone just *stopped* working? Then when you called your cell-phone company they told you to remove the battery and look for a "white" dot? Oh, so the white dot is pink? Or red? Which is it?

According to your cell-phone company, the fact that your white dot turned pink or red means you got the phone wet. This means your warranty is now voided. But how accurate are these moisture-detecting dots, really? According to one cell-phone repair shop, they're not accurate all. In fact, just living in a humid climate could trigger the "moisture strip" to turn from white to red.

If your cell phone has stopped working, and the little white strip in the battery compartment is no longer white, what can you do about it? Visit eBay.com and search for "Moisture Strips in Cell Phones," then buy a set of replacement dots for a few dollars that you can put into your phone before calling tech support.

YOUR CELL-PHONE COMPANY AND YOU (PART FIVE): THEY SAY YOU'RE A "MOTOR MOUTH"

All those phone calls you make to Aunt Mary and your best, best friend add up in the course of a month. But, are you really talking *that* much? Sure, you may have won first place for "Heaviest Cell Phone Usage" once, but you probably really don't use as many minutes as these guys say you do. They overwhelm you with all the details of how they bill: six-second billing, one-minute charges for incomplete calls, and ten cents for each of the first one hundred text messages. Who has time to research and study all of this stuff? Better yet, who has the inclination to make sure these monsters are living up to their billing standards?

It's time to face the music: They're not always honest and you have to find creative ways to beat them at their game of "Bait and Hook." (If we're not careful, they'll feed the most gullible of us to their sharks.)

Now, before you continue, I would suggest grabbing a stiff drink and isolating yourself for at least an hour, because what you're about to read will make you *insanely angry*!

In the Yankee Group 2006 Mobile User Study, people with wireless contracts reported *paying* for 791 minutes per month, but in reality, they were only *using* 477 of those minutes every month.

Bottom line: If you're an average cell-phone user, then you are probably paying 40% *more* for your wireless minutes than you think you are. How does that make you feel? Pretty used, doesn't it? And if you're an especially *good* customer, you're probably punching holes in your wall at the moment.

Welcome to the "good life" of customer service. There's nothing customary about it. It's all designed to screw you and protect them.

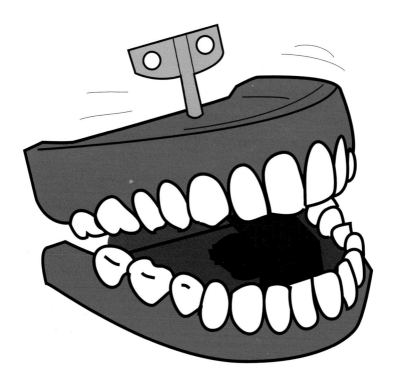

CULPRIT: Yeah, it's the cell-phone company (again).

PROBLEM: Dishonest pricing schemes

THE HOME RUN: It's a pay-as-go cellular plan that keeps the bullies honest and on a "cellular diet." Otherwise, you'll always be an adjustment away from being nickel-and-dimed to eke out more money for your cell carrier.

"But wait!" you say. "Even if I save money every month with a pay-as-you-go plan, don't I have to pay a huge sum of money to get out of the contract I currently have?" Maybe, but the best way to know for sure if you can get that big cellular company out of your wallet or purse is to sit down and do the math:

- How many months are left in your contract?
- How many unused minutes do you have left each month?
- How much will it cost you to get out of your existing cell plan?
- How much will you save each month by going to a "pay-as-you-go" plan?

This is by far the surest way to keep the cell-phone vampires at bay. Good luck.

YOUR CELL-PHONE CARRIER AND YOU (PART SIX): DEALING WITH CARRIERS OTHER THAN MA BELL

There are several wireless carriers in North America that are willing to offer service to anyone (even if they're barely breathing). Let's say Ma Bell is rolling out another new iPhone today (iPhone 4G, perhaps?) and the media and the public are obsessing over the phone like the world is ending tomorrow. However, you are not necessarily interested in the phone, but a decent deal on a top-shelf phone that's offered by your carrier. What can you do?

CULPRIT: The wireless company that isn't Ma Bell

PROBLEM: You think you can't get a better phone from your carrier.

A CLEVER WAY OF GETTING A GOOD DEAL ON A BETTER PHONE: Right before the rollout begins, call your cell-phone company and say:

"I've been checking out those new iPhones online and they look really *cool! I've been thinking about canceling my account with your company and going to Ma Bell and getting one, but if you'll agree to give me one of your top-of-the-line phones right now, I will stay here and sign a new two-year contract with you, instead."*

BONUS! You've got to time this call to your cellular carrier just right, because if the new iPhone is selling really well on launch day, that gives you more leverage to demand more stuff for free. But if the new iPhone isn't selling well, you may lose the leverage you need to get all the free stuff you want.

YOUR CELL-PHONE CARRIER AND YOU (PART SEVEN): ESCAPING THE BONDAGE OF "CONTRACT HELL"

So you've convinced yourself that you really, really want an iPhone. You can't resist that everyone and their dog has one. Nor can you deny its sleek, sexy design. I'll be first to admit that it's a great phone, but . . . it's not perfect. Like all corporations, cell-phone companies are in business to do one thing: Make money! What does this mean? They'll do whatever's necessary to keep the profits flowing, which is one reason cell-phone companies have in place a glorious "legal document" better known as a contract.

CULPRIT: The contract-obsessed cell-phone carriers

PROBLEM: Avoiding their contractual obligations

GETTING OUT OF THE "CONTRACTUAL DANCE": Instead of buying your phone from the carrier, buy a used iPhone at www.nextworth.com instead. Here's why this is a better idea: If you *don't* buy your iPhone from an official retailer, you won't have to sign a two-year contract and you can use the phone on any compatible cellular carrier in the world that you want.

BONUS! Anyone who is seriously considering buying a new phone should compare the features of the new model to the features of the previous model before buying. Why?

Because it may be that for you the new features will not be of any great additional use or value. Therefore, there's no sense locking yourself into a new two-year contract when the previous generation of iPhone would be perfect for you, and you can get one online and use it without signing any kind of contract at all.

For example, when the second-generation iPhone 3G debuted, the most exciting two new features on the phone were access to the faster 3G network for Web surfing, and built-in GPS. But for many people, these new features weren't very valuable since they didn't live or work where there was reliable access to the faster 3G network and/or they didn't really live a lifestyle where having GPS would often be helpful.

CREATIVE TACTICS TO ATTRACT PUBLICITY (WITHOUT A PR AGENCY)

The public relations (PR) industry is the engine of publicity. Unfortunately, the services they provide aren't cheap, and rightfully so. These guys are skilled copywriters, "image managers," and networkers. Essentially, you're paying for their experience and clout.

If you just recently launched a business, have an idea, or are considering a project that could use a little publicity, then chances are you may lack the budget to afford a top-notch PR agency. This is okay. Fortunately, there are ways to get press coverage without an agency or without spending money.

Too good to be true? It's not!

My first taste of publicity was in 1995 when I competed in a national high school computer programming competition in Atlanta, Georgia. We would later be featured in a magazine for our first place ranking, of which we were all very proud. I've since been featured or quoted by the *Detroit News*, *TechCrunch*, the *Associated Press*, *The Christian Science Monitor*, the *Nashville Business Journal*, the *Denver Post*, the *Boulder County Business Report*, and dozens of other media—all without the help of a PR agency.

How did I do it? I'm glad you asked! Here are a few ideas to save a little money on PR until you're able to afford their services.

CULPRIT: The expense of PR agencies

PROBLEM: You don't have enough pennies to pay for their services.

GET CREATIVE AND LAND SOME PUBLICITY: The first thing you *must* know is this: a positive mindset is absolutely required to attract publicity without a PR agency! Secondly, you must believe in what you're pitching, regardless of how many times you're rejected or passed over for coverage. Sure, it's okay to feel disappointed, but don't make a habit of feeling bad about it, okay?

Now that the important notices are out of the way, let's focus on how to get some press for your new whiz-bang gadget or idea. One thing to keep in mind is that there's an unlimited amount of opportunities to lure attention in your direction. Drill this into your head. Don't forget it! Now, let's get some press:

GO "FISHING" AT LOCAL NEWSPAPERS. I landed coverage of my new business in the *Detroit News* by calling up their business writers and inquiring about upcoming stories. Ask around and talk to people about stories that might be relevant to what you're doing. Also, be sure to mention what you're up to as well. In doing this, I managed to get my mug on the front page of the *News'* Business section.

READ A LOT OF PRESS RELEASES—THEN EMULATE. I'll admit that I don't know diddly about writing press releases. However, I've always had a penchant for following the news of many companies and I had a habit of reading their press releases, too. The first press release I wrote (distributed by *BusinessWire*) was about the move of a new company I started from Detroit to Nashville. I targeted its release exclusively to the Nashville media and the strategy worked! Nashville's top business paper—*The Nashville Business Journal*—did an impressive write-up about my new business experiment, Edub. I received dozens of phone calls plus interest from as far away as Oregon. Taking ideas from all the press releases I've read, along with reading the basics of how a press release is written, I managed to write a press release that delivered! You can do the same.

BE "FIRST"—THEN "PING" MAJOR BLOGS. When I discovered that Google had mistakenly increased the storage of my Gmail inbox to more than 15GB, I immediately performed a screen capture, opened up Photoshop, and doodled around to create a decent illustration of the snafu. I knew right away that this was a newsworthy event, so I uploaded the illustration to Flickr (www.flickr.com), typed a short description, and linked it to my new blog entry. After everything was done, I pinged all the major Google-related blogs and created a firestorm of discussion around the storage increase. The details surrounding this oddity are still unknown today, but the PR ride was great!

"HELP A REPORTER." The easiest way on the planet to attract publicity! Peter Shankman's HARO (www.helpareporter.com) is an exclusive, free e-mail list of impressive queries from *Newsweek*, Dr. Phil, the *Wall Street Journal*, and many other major media outlets. Shankman sends out an e-mail three times each day—with the exception of weekends and major holidays.

Once you're signed up, find a press query that strikes your fancy and respond! If they're interested, you'll be contacted. Pretty simple, eh? Now that you have a few ideas on how to attract publicity for yourself, what will you do next? How about getting some coverage? Good luck!

THE WALLED GARDEN OF APPLE (PART ONE): IPOD AND ITUNES

When Apple developed the iPod and iTunes, the company knew it was creating a platform that would print blank checks for many years to come. However, this isn't really about the fact that Apple enjoys caging its consumers like gorillas (we'd hope not anyway, right?), but like any company that's focused on producing profits, it must develop products which *perform*.

What does this mean to the average consumer? You're

stuck, buddy! No pouting allowed! No tantrums. Nada. Sometimes, we must pay the ultimate price for the gadgets we often obsess over: A lack of freedom. You would expect to have such freedom with a product you own, but that isn't how many companies think. They want you to abide by their terms, even though you plunked down a few hundred bucks to acquire the goods.

So, how do you break free of Apple? When can you tell your friends that you're finally free? I thought you'd never ask! Let's explore some options, shall we?

Next to your cell phone, what's the second "most-likely-to-be-on-your-person" piece of technology in your life? That's right . . . your iPod. But that being said, here's why most people don't keep or have all their songs in iTunes. If Apple had their way, they'd lock you up in their own music and video prison and never you let you out. By that I mean:

They'd make it impossible for you to buy songs for your iPod from anywhere but iTunes.

They'd make it impossible for you to get your songs off your iPod and into any other brand of MP3 player.

CULPRIT: The world's most recognized consumer electronics company

PROBLEM: Lack of music freedom

ESCAPE CAMP APPLE AT ITUNES: SharePod is an easy and free system that allows you to add and remove music and videos from your iPod, copy materials from your iPod to PC, and more. Go to getsharepod.com

THE WALLED GARDEN OF APPLE (PART TWO): DOWNLOADING MOVIES BEYOND ITUNES

So you went out and spent a bunch of money on a new iPod Touch or iPhone (a.k.a. "Jesus Touch" and "Jesus Phone"). How does it feel? You're probably overjoyed. You're also looking forward to using that big, beautiful widescreen display to watch some of your favorite movies that you already own as well.

Unfortunately, it doesn't work that way. In the Apple/iPod/iPhone world, the only movies you get to watch on your iPod or iPhone are movies that you buy from Apple and iTunes. Yes, corporations aren't always focused on the consumer—only themselves (again, it's about those record earnings and pleasing their stakeholders first).

Well, it's time to take matters into your own hands!

CULPRIT: Stifling electronics giant

PROBLEM: Lack of freedom to load whatever movie you want onto your iPhone

HOW TO WATCH WHATEVER MOVIE YOUR HEART DESIRES:

- Go to www.handbrake.fr and download the "GUI" version of the free software ("GUI" stands for "Graphical User Interface").
- Install Handbrake on your computer.
- Put a DVD into your computer's DVD drive.
- Launch Handbrake and follow the instructions.

THE WALLED GARDEN OF APPLE (PART THREE): PROTECTING YOUR MUSIC COLLECTION

In a world of apples and oranges, fruits are perishable and their shelf life is limited. The same is true for the lifespan of your music.

Why? Because, first, all your songs live on your computer. And then you move them all to your iPod. But do you have a backup copy of all your songs? You may *think* you do, but you *probably* don't. The reason why is that most people who own iPods think that because they have copies of all their music in two places (computer, iPod), they have, in essence, a backup copy of all their music. This simply isn't true.

Let's examine. If your iPod suddenly dies, you lose it, you chew it up for dinner, or you drop and break it, you can certainly buy a new iPod and reload it with all the music from your computer again. But what if your computer's hard drive crashes and burns? All it takes is a catastrophic event for it to fail and you're doomed beyond repair and can't recover your data! Oh, heavens, no!

So, what are your options?

CULPRIT: Faulty computer

PROBLEM: No sure backup plan for your music

A SOUND SOLUTION TO KEEPING YOUR MUSIC: The cheapest, easiest and most reliable way to back up a computer is with a company called Carbonite (www. Carbonite.com). Carbonite and its competitors provide Internet-based file and synchronization services for a modest monthly fee. What's a couple of bucks for peace of mind?

If your computer does end up crashing and you don't have a fail-safe backup plan, you might be in luck:

- Without plugging your iPod into your new computer, reinstall iTunes and sign in to your account.

- Go to www.kennettnet.co.uk and get a free trial copy of their Music Rescue software.

- Plug your iPod into your computer.

- Watch as the software magically copies all the files from your iPod onto your computer.

- Show your appreciation by going back to the Music Rescue site and paying about $20 for the software that just saved your $10,000 music collection.

OH, CANADA: EXTENDING YOUR STAY WITHOUT DOCUMENTATION OR HASSLE

WARNING: Do NOT attempt to circumvent Canada's immigration rules and laws! Doing so could lead to your permanent expulsion from North America's second-best country.

For twenty-one years, Windsor, Ontario, was minutes away from my doorstep in Detroit, Michigan. For reasons I cannot explain, I rarely visited Detroit's Canadian neighbor. It was only after leaving Detroit that I would maintain a frequent presence in the country (mainly Alberta, but also British Columbia)—including a six-month stay (as granted by my visa documentation). You must follow the rules, eh?

Canada is always a thrill to visit, whether by air or ground. From the beautiful greens in Vancouver to the rugged terrain of the Canadian Rockies, Canada is truly a majestic and inspiring country. However, Canada's border-crossing procedures are imperfect—even flawed. If you're creative, you could probably sneak in a few cows, chickens, refugees, cars, mobile homes, and ex-girlfriends.

You might be wondering, "What if someone was attempting to enter the country illegally or to spend more time than legally allowed?" Continue reading to find out how they'd do it.

CULPRIT: Lax border-crossing rules

PROBLEM: You could wear out your welcome—and get in trouble, too.

STAYING LONGER THAN PLANNED IN A GREAT COUNTRY: Because Canada is a relatively small country in population (approximately 40 million), compared to America, it lacks the personnel to effectively manage its border, which means security breaches and extended stays are very possible. For example, when crossing the border between Detroit and Windsor, Canadian officials are known for *not* asking for your proof of citizenship or inquiring about the term of your visit.

What does this mean? Well, you don't have to prove anything about why you're visiting or where you're going. It means that without documentation, you could in effect stay indefinitely if you were attempting to flee prosecution in the United States, an abusive spouse, or taxation. Or, if you have a girlfriend or boyfriend in the country, and you desire to stay a week or two beyond your visa's limit, you could probably pull it off! After all, you're practically free to roam the country as long as you wish—all without proper knowledge other than a face-to-face conversation during your time of entry.

I've visited Canada enough times by air and ground to observe these border imperfections with great clarity and alarm. Yet, due to my brutal honesty, I've never taken advantage of crossings where I wasn't given documentation, but here are some of Canada's most relaxed and strict border crossings (depending upon agent, traffic, and other variables, of course):

EASY (NOT ALWAYS GUARANTEED):

- Windsor, Ontario, Canada
- Buffalo, New York
- Vancouver, British Columbia

HARD (NOT ALWAYS GUARANTEED):

- Coutts, Alberta (often very strict, unpleasant personalities at times)

REMEMBER: Don't get any crazy ideas! Respect the country and it will respect you!

BIG-BOX RETAILERS AND YOU: GETTING A BETTER DEAL YOU CAN LIVE WITH

The "300-Pound Gorilla" in electronics retail is easily identifiable in the United States and Canada by its bright yellow price-tag logo and blue exterior. In North America, we often drool over the thousands of products they carry, fantasizing about the number of pennies we can stack up to afford the shiny new widescreen TV, fancy desk chair, or high-powered microwave to nuke gourmet hotdogs in high-class fashion.

Like any retail behemoth, these guys have a talented workforce focused on one thing: selling you all the extras like insurance and warranties. It's the equivalent of walking into a restaurant and being asked to upgrade your combo to include a larger drink and fries (as if we *really* need the extras!).

So, how can you get a better deal?

CULPRIT: Annoying retail employees

PROBLEM: Extras you don't really need

PLAYING THEIR GAME AND GETTING WHAT YOU WANT: In their training, there has been great emphasis put on how to *up-sell*, or how to sell people more stuff like *extra services* and *extra accessories*. So when you walk in to buy a new computer, they try to sell you an extended warranty and a new printer and a new monitor and a universal backup system. And when you walk in to buy a new big-screen TV, they try to sell you an $800 installation package and a "special" set of $300 cables.

But here's what you can do to get a deal: take it all! No matter what the salesperson offers, take it:

↳ The overpriced cables!

↳ The overpriced installation!

↳ The overpriced extended warranty!

Next, after you agree to buy all this stuff, look the salesperson square in the eye and say:

"Thanks for suggesting that I buy all this extra stuff, because if you hadn't recommended it, I wouldn't have known that I needed it. And here's one more thing I want to ask you about. Now that I've bought both the computer/TV/camera AND all this extra stuff, can you give me an extra 20% discount on the actual computer/TV/camera?"

Then once you negotiate the new price on your computer/TV/camera, go stand in line without the salesperson and when you get to the register tell the cashier that you changed your mind about all the extra stuff and that you only want the computer/TV/camera (which has been marked down because of your superior negotiation skills).

COMPUTER SOFTWARE AND YOU: FINDING ALTERNATIVES TO MICROSOFT

It seems the entire world runs on Microsoft software. Bill Gates' vision of a "computer on every desk and in every home" is more than a reality today: gas pumps, PDAs, and possibly fish tanks are running the company's software. It's all rather mind-boggling once you think about it. Indeed, we've become a "Microsoft world."

Yet, there are great alternatives to Microsoft software— and this coming from a former Microsoft fan-boy who drank all of the "Microsoft Kool-Aid" and was a top volunteer beta tester among many other things.

So, what are the alternatives?

CULPRIT: Microsoft

PROBLEM: Their software is everywhere we are.

THE OTHER SOFTWARE OPTIONS:

Internet Browsing—If you're comfortable with animals, you might consider the world's most extensible, safest, and customizable Web browser around: Firefox. Grab the fox by its tail at www.mozilla.org/firefox.

Productivity—Microsoft Office isn't the only productivity suite around. You can use comparable and compatible and free products such as Google Docs (docs.google.com) or the open source office package called OpenOffice (www.openoffice.org).

Operating Systems—The best modern operating system Microsoft has released to date is Windows XP. Vista, on the other hand, is far worse than a Nightmare on Elm Street—Freddy Krueger himself is frightened by the train wreck this piece of software is. Bypass Vista and wait for Microsoft's next-generation operating system. It should be everything Vista isn't.

If you're feeling adventurous, try the Linux operating system (developed by Linus Torvalds). It's delivered via various distributions, with some of the most popular being Redhat (www.redhat.com), OpenSuse (www.opensuse.org), and Ubuntu (www.ubuntu.com).

GOOD-BYE MICROSOFT AND APPLE: HELLO LINUX AND NETBOOKS

Like the average human being, you're probably a Mac or PC user. Your "computer religion" is chosen for you as Mac OS X or Windows. The combination of the software and hardware make for great premiums at Microsoft, Apple, and the cash register ("computer tithes").

But what if you also bemoan paying so much for their computers and software? Is there a solution? Yes!

CULPRIT: The usual corporate computing offerings

PROBLEM: The expense of the average PC or Mac

SMASHING THE COST OF COMPUTING: In recent years a new category of inexpensive laptops has hit the market that are called "Netbooks" and one reason they're inexpensive is because they're offered with Linux—a completely free operating system.

Because these computers are already designed to perform an end run around the grasp Microsoft maintains on the computer industry, it turns out that it becomes much easier to also use the machines to perform an end run around the "Apple problem," too.

The end result is that you can buy one of these "Netbooks" for less than $300 and turn it into a Mac. Compare this with the lowest-priced Mac laptop at the time of this writing, which is $1,300. The choice is clear, but it ultimately depends on your needs and requirements.

Want to know more? The process required to convert a Netbook to a Mac is complicated and it requires some patience and technical expertise. *Wired* magazine provides a comprehensive guide to make the conversion: http://howto.wired.com/wiki/Run_Mac_OS_X_on_a_Netbook.

DITCHING YOUR COMPUTER COMPANY AFTER THE PURCHASE

When it comes to computers, companies like to think that once you buy their computers they can trick you into thinking they're your only option for parts and accessories, too. However, this simply isn't true!

So how do you skate around the heads of these manipulators? It's pretty simple.

CULPRIT: The "one-stop shop" computer company

PROBLEM: Their overpriced products

AVOID THE GAME AND SAVE YOURSELF SOME MONEY:

Laptop Batteries—The problem with buying a replacement battery for your laptop is that once your laptop dies, the brand-new battery becomes useless to you, too.

So here's a better solution: Go to your favorite electronics or office retailer and buy a one-size-fits-all universal laptop battery. The reason for doing so is that you'll be able to use this universal laptop battery with your current laptop, your future laptop, and the laptops of all your friends and family members, too.

Docking Stations—Sure, it's great to throw your laptop onto the super expensive, matching docking station that the laptop manufacturer offers, which allows you to keep a keyboard, mouse, and monitor, and lots of other accessories plugged in and ready to go, but the reality is that these docking stations are expensive accessories that you end up tossing every time you replace your laptop.

So, here's a better idea: If you buy a universal one-size-fits-all USB docking station, you continue using it with your current laptop and any future laptops you may buy. This means you can pass it on to a friend, family member, or some yet unborn child who might use a computer when they're of age.

Replacement memory and hard drives—What your laptop company doesn't want you to know is that these parts are standardized, so you can get them from many sources (Newegg.com, Crucial.com) and often at half the price your laptop company sells them for.

GETTING RID OF THE GARBAGE ON YOUR NEW COMPUTER: A PRIMER ON "CRAPWARE"

You buy a new computer and you expect it to run well because, well, it's new. It shouldn't require an entire year to boot up your shiny new toy, nor should you be bothered by an endless amount of pop-ups, barking dogs, and other nonsense you won't use.

But it doesn't run well and you can't figure out why. The problem is called "crapware."

This is tons of stupid free software or trial software that computer manufacturers get paid by other companies to pre-install on their computers. It's another way of making more money for themselves while making you suffer as the end user. Who are these guys for anyway? Oh, right, it's not you! Of course, they're hoping you'll fall in love with this crap and actually agree to pay for it when the trial period ends. Surprise! You don't fall in love with the garbage and you just live with it because you probably don't know it's there or how to get rid of it.

It's that time again. It's time to find a solution in the midst of chaos.

CULPRIT: Profit-obsessed computer company

PROBLEM: More "crapware" than a virtual landfill can hold

HOW TO RESTORE YOUR COMPUTER TO ACTUALLY ACT LIKE A NEW ONE: Mostly, "crapware" is a Windows problem and your new computer should have come with a Windows disk or "Operating System" disk. To get rid of all the "crapware" on your brand-new computer, you will need to reformat the hard drive and then reinstall the operating system before doing anything else.

The disk you'll need is normally labeled as "System Restore" or something similar. Some even offer a range of options to customize the restore. Just hope that yours is customizable, because there's still a possibility that they'll load up your computer with the same crap.

You can also try using what's called a "PC Decrapifier." This won't get rid of everything, but it's easy and fast. Go to pcdecrapifier.com to use it.

THE FEDERAL RESERVE: FORCING THE WORLD'S MOST SECRETIVE CROOKS INTO A CORNER (AND TAKING BACK WHAT'S YOURS!)

Prior to 1913, America was truly a free republic (don't pay any attention to the malarkey about it being a "democracy" now—that's a bowl of horse's soup). It didn't have trillions of dollars in debt nor was its currency printed out of thin air. The pre–Federal Reserve era of America was a sensible nation based on practical approaches to currency creation and social prosperity.

Today, we should be reminded of how much has changed in the land of the enslaved—yes, the enslaved:

The Great Depression of 1929, orchestrated by the Federal Reserve, rocked America's promise and created much suffering throughout the land.

Since 1913, the Federal Reserve has devalued the dollar by 95%—hence the stories of candy bars costing five cents during your great-grandparents' generation.

Most Americans today are indebted to banks in the form of loans with interest (which simply grows the coffers of the greedy elite).

I will not spend much time covering the history of the Federal Reserve—instead, I'd like to encourage you to do this yourself. There are plenty of videos on YouTube, documents, and other material that will bring you up to speed on this unconstitutional, private corporation. Yes, that's right, *private*!

You see, for many years, the elite banking families were obsessed with regaining control of America, a land that was freed from British rule thanks to the infamous Declaration of Independence in 1776. It was this proclamation, partly inspired by the unjust and foreign taxation of the original thirteen colonies, which led the colonists to devise a path to independence from monetary slavery. As mentioned in countless history books, they succeeded!

Unfortunately, America is no longer a free nation, contrary to what the people are told by their government and mass media. Like sheep grazing on dirt, the people are often misguided, lied to, and manipulated to accept this fraudulent reality about how money works in America. It's a very, very sad fact and one that has proven difficult to reverse.

Here's why the Federal Reserve is *unconstitutional*, as stated by the constitution in Article I, Section 8:

"The Congress shall have Power… to coin Money, regulate the Value thereof, and of foreign Coin, and fix the Standard of Weights and Measures."

Now, ask yourself this question: Why is a "pseudo-Federal" establishment coining and regulating our currency? Why are only a chosen few within the Fed allowed to see its books, owners, and procedures? Congress is granted these rights under the Constitution, but instead has deferred them to a secret and private corporation that answers to no one—not even the president of the United States.

Does this make sense to you? It shouldn't! It's akin to buying a house and allowing another family to live in it while you find shelter at a friend's or family member's home. It's absurd and America has paid dearly for this arrangement in the price of record deficits and debt—all mostly created from a reality-based game of Monopoly. The monetary policies set by the Federal Reserve are no different than a gathering of friends around a game of Monopoly. The banker is no different than the Fed's chairman. Both are make-believe game players.

Ready to make a difference and take back America from selfish, power-obsessed individuals?

CULPRIT: A careless government

PROBLEM: A private corporation that controls the people through imaginary money

RESOLVING TO DEMOLISH PERPETUAL, MONETARY SLAVERY: There's a growing number of Americans who are waking up to the lie of the Federal Reserve Act of 1913 thanks to Ron Paul, Peter Schiff, Alex Jones, and many others. Through their tireless efforts, individuals and organizations are speaking out against the Federal Reserve and the reckless economic policies of the U.S. government—and they're making a difference!

You, too, can make a difference by understanding the rights granted to you by reading or refreshing yourself about the constitution. An informed mind is a powerful mind. When you're ready to fight the good fight, here are a few organizations you should consider joining:

- We Are Change (www.wearechange.org)
- Campaign for Liberty (www.campaignforliberty.org)
- Restore the Republic (www.restoretherepublic.com)

A good book that educates the people and exposes the Federal Reserve is *Web of Debt: The Shocking Truth About Our Monetary System and How We Can Break Free* by Ellen Hodgson Brown, J.D. Visit www.webofdebt.com for details, blog posts, videos, and more. Don't believe the hype. Question the fat suits in Congress and behind the curtain. Question everything.

THE POWER OF FREE SOFTWARE (PART ONE): HOW ONE MAN REINVENTED THE TELEPHONE AND THE WAY WE COMMUNICATE

If you're a CEO, consultant, or business owner, then you're well aware of one of the first things to do after incorporating your business: Establish phone service!

The telephone, one of the world's best inventions, developed by Alexander Graham Bell, has made the world smaller over the last century or so. Humanity has shared many firsts with each other over the wires: a newborn baby's cry, words of love and encouragement, and the agony of learning that your 401K is in the toilet.

However, a lot has changed since the invention of the telephone. We evolved from pulse dialing to tone dialing and from clunky rotary dials to push-button phones. They've changed shape, functionality, and design. It's a bare necessity for keeping in touch.

CULPRIT: A few empires controlling how human beings communicate by phone

PROBLEM: Little choice, little freedom

SETTING THE WORLD FREE OF THE TELEPHONE MONOPOLIES: 1999 was the year of change for the telephone and how we used it—something many weren't prepared for. A young college student, Mark Spencer, couldn't afford a $5,000 phone system to run his new business, Linux Support Services in Huntsville, Alabama. After all, where's a college student going to get this money from? It's not like every kid has a piggy bank that could be broken to release one's long-forgotten riches. Instead, Spencer had a better plan: Make your own phone system!

Spencer had previous software development experience, along with internships at Adtran, a major telecommunications supplier. Using Linux, he hacked together a vanilla phone system that, while imperfect and quirky, was able to meet the early needs of his business. Later, he recognized an opportunity: Why not allow other people to develop it as well?

Spencer would soon release the first code of his new private branch exchange (PBX) software, Asterisk. A free and open source (anyone is free to contribute code), Asterisk grew like a wildfire. Millions of downloads (and dollars) later, Digium—the new company Spencer launched in 2002—has experienced tremendous success in the telecommunications industry.

What's so beautiful about Asterisk? You can save thousands of dollars compared to similar PBX systems offered by Cisco, Avaya, and Nortel. It has voice mail, conferencing, caller ID, and all the features we've grown to use and love in the office and at home. Overnight, Asterisk has freed enthusiasts to communicate freely and openly by bypassing the monopoly of the "old guard." Now, anyone can easily program extensions, add phone numbers, and more without requiring permission from the company. How cool is that?

Before you start evaluating all your phone-system options, be sure to give Asterisk a try. If traditional phone guys are leaving behind the Mitels and Avayas of the world for this open platform, then it's obvious there's some incredible value in Asterisk. All it requires is a simple PC, Internet access, Linux, and a "network-enabled phone." In just under an hour, you, too, can pretend to have the phone presence of a major company for zero cost.

The ingenuity and imagination of Spencer has enabled an ecosystem that effectively allows everyday people to play with "big telephone toys" for free. His development of the Asterisk PBX has more than proven its effectiveness as a "telephony toolbox"—it has his largest competitors shaking with fear over the growth of his telephone platform.

To try Asterisk for yourself, visit www.asterisk.org. And after you've kicked the tires for a bit and feel confident enough to try it for yourself, head over to Amazon Web Services (aws.amazon.com) and create an account to load the software on a pre-built Linux server (if you don't already have a PC to dedicate to Linux) to get up and running with ease.

There are always options to work around expensive old-guard solutions. Always.

THE POWER OF FREE SOFTWARE (PART TWO): HOW GOOGLE BUILT A MULTIBILLION-DOLLAR EMPIRE

Who said there isn't a thing such as a free lunch? Try telling this to Google founders Sergey Brin and Larry Page. Together in 1999, they launched what would become the world's largest and most successful Internet company— later trumping Internet pioneers such as Yahoo, AltaVista, and Excite!

The secret to Brin's and Page's success can be described in two ways:

- Teamwork and great research built an innovative search engine
- Creative application of free software built a successful business

For those who are technologically savvy, you may already be aware that Google built its business on Linux—the free and open operating system that's witnessed billions of dollars in investments from Intel, IBM, Redhat, and other major companies. Instead of opting for a Microsoft solution, Brin and Page developed the backbone of their company on mostly free software—saving possibly millions of dollars in the process.

Ready to tinker around with the same software Google built its business on?

CULPRIT: Overpriced software

PROBLEM: Little money left over to grow a new idea

CREATING THE NEXT BIG IDEA FROM FREE SOFTWARE:
The success of free software is visible all around the
world. Your favorite Web sites and tools are most likely
powered by Linux and a suite of open-source software like
MySQL (a database platform equivalent to Microsoft's
SQL Server), Apache (a standards-based web server),
and WordPress (a modern-day "software press" for our
times). Like Google, or some of the most successful Web
sites on the Internet, you too can use the same tools to
build the next big idea.

To try this software for yourself, download it free of
charge:

- Linux—Ubuntu (the most popular "Linux distribution")—
  www.ubuntu.com

- MySQL ("the Internet's database server")—www.
  mysql.com

- Apache—("the Internet's Web server")—www.apache.org

THROWING OUT THE COMPANY BEHIND YOUR COMPUTER WARRANTY

When it comes to computers, now is the time to tell you the truth. Computer manufacturers are always looking for ways to boost profit margins. What does this mean to you? Quality-wise, it probably doesn't matter which brand of computer you buy (unless you're buying a high-end machine), because most of them are built from cheap components and plastics.

So, when you're buying a new computer, here's the #1 thing that matters most: the quality and duration of the warranty. Particularly if you are using the computer for school or work and *really* need it every day, then you should spend more time comparing warranties than you do comparing prices of the machines themselves.

And if you do mission-critical work on your computer, here's what you should look for in a warranty or extended warranty for additional cost:

- A laptop warranty that includes screen replacement even if you break the screen by dropping the laptop or by some other accidental means
- A warranty that includes on-site service at your home or office
- A warranty that guarantees service within a short, specified period of time like twenty-four or forty-eight hours

And here's the next thing you need to know: When you have computer problems, the company from which you bought the warranty will do *anything* to avoid sending out an expensive technician to fix your machine, even though you specifically bought the machine because it had a superior warranty, and maybe you even paid extra for the better warranty. In fact, in an effort to avoid having to send the expensive technician to your home or office to do an on-site repair, your computer company will try to keep you on the phone for hours trying to figure out a way for you to diagnose and repair the problem yourself.

Fortunately, boys and girls, you *can* get what you paid for *and* more.

CULPRIT: The ultra-cheap computer manufacturer

PROBLEM: Dirt bag warranty tactics

THE BEST WAY TO DEAL WITH THIS SITUATION: When you call for service or to report a problem, tell them about the symptoms you are experiencing, but also tell them you can't even get the computer to turn on anymore (unfortunately, you might be forced to tell a "white lie," because, after all, are they being honest with you?).

By telling them the computer doesn't work, you have just made it impossible for them to waste a lot of your time trying to diagnose the problem over the phone. Instead, they will *have* to send a technician out to fix the problem, and when he or she gets there, they will see that you have somehow, miraculously, gotten the machine to power up again.

KEEPING THE PRINTER COMPANY OFF YOUR BACK AND IN CHECK

Imagine this: You're driving down the highway, listening to your favorite music and throwing bananas out the window at stray dogs. Suddenly, a light on your dash tells you that it's time for you to buy more gas. You pull off at the next exit, go to the nearest gas station, and, even though you've still got a quarter-tank of gas, the gas station requires that you dump it out and completely refill your gas tank.

Now, that's absurd.

But it's not so absurd that HP, Canon, Kodak, Epson, and Lexmark don't tell us to do the same thing with our print cartridges every day. You know the routine: You get an error message on your printer that says it's out of ink, even though the last page printed looked great. Now, it won't allow you to print at all, until you throw a new one of those $30 print cartridges into the printer.

Don't you just feel screwed when this happens? After all, you can tell by looking at the last page you printed that there's still a ton of ink left in the cartridge.

Why won't the dog continue working until it has exhausted its reserve of ink? Because it's been programmed to stop printing while there's a ton of ink still left for the obvious reason that if it tells you that the ink cartridge is empty *and* you can't keep printing, you're going to go buy more cartridges and feed it more ink.

Disgusting, or what? You have probably wondered if this was what was going on. You have probably cursed those greedy printer executives under your breath. And here's your confirmation that it's true based on research done by *PC World* magazine. So what can you do about it?

First off, shed some tears for all the ink you've already paid for and flushed down the drain, because *PC World's* test shows that on average the printer companies are using sneaky tricks to force us to throw away as much as *half* of all the ink we pay for. Aren't you ready to dance on their heads and make them change their ways?

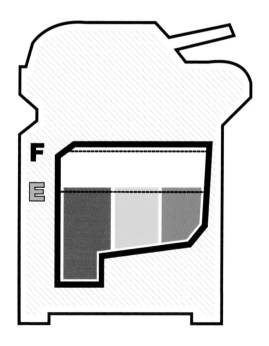

Next, let this next statistic motivate you to do something about it:

If you use a gallon of ink over the life of your printer, it will cost you as much as $4,731.

So now how do you feel about your printer company forcing you to throw as much as half of your ink away?

There is, of course, something you can do about it.

CULPRIT: Money-munching printer manufacturers

PROBLEM: The habitual lies their printers tell us

REFILLING YOUR WAY TO SAVINGS: In some cases, you can "trick" your printer cartridge into thinking that it still has ink, by coloring in a little window with a black Sharpie, or sticking a piece of duct tape over a hole.

But how will you know what to do? Use Google, of course, to find the trick that applies to your particular printer. You can start by doing searches using keywords like this:

- Printer brand and model number
- Ink cartridge hack

And what if there is *no* trick to be found? Go to the store (or visit their Web site), pick out a few printers you like, and then go home and Google them to make sure there's a trick you can use for the next printer you buy.

The bottom line: Give up on the fact that you already spent perfectly good money on the printer you have. If the company that made it insists on screwing you over and over again by demanding that you need more ink when your tank is half full, then it's time to toss the printer and cut them off from their form of "abusive welfare."

"WINNING A ROUND OF BOXING" WITH THE BIG-BOX RETAILERS

Price protection. Most of the big-box stores offer this snazzy "feature" as part of their retail experience. While there are many purposes, the primary one is to drive traffic through their doors and convince you to buy something! Let's say you buy something expensive, and you know that if the price goes down at that store or one of the competing stores within fourteen or thirty days, they'll refund you the difference plus 10%, or some crazy thing like that.

The only thing is that it's not so crazy, because if there was an easy way to keep track of the prices, it could translate into cold, hard cash in your pocket. We all like extra money, right? Well, here's something you'll enjoy:

While you're standing in the store, you're probably thinking to yourself that you will certainly watch the prices go down, and you will certainly go back to the store and get your extra money. I mean, why not, right? But when was the last time you actually did it? It's probably been years, because even though it's your money if you do the work to get it, for most of us it's too much of a pain to do the work and actually go and get it.

Well, this is the "gotcha" of price protection. The big-box guys are masters at doing little things that we'll later forget about. That's exactly why stores offer price protection, because they know the "protection" will motivate most of us to stop shopping and to buy right now, even though most of us will never go back to get the extra cash.

Is there a way around the hassle of price protection? Is it possible to line the pockets that were once bulging with cash prior to your big-box visit? Surprisingly, yes!

CULPRIT: Big-box retailer and "price protection"

PROBLEM: Tracking the pricing of merchandise for a refund

BEST SOLUTION: www.PriceProtectr.com

Open a free account, enter the items you have recently purchased and their price, and the Web site will send you an e-mail when the price drops and you are due a refund. The next step is quite simple. You must decide if you will collect the difference or allow the monkey to walk away with what's rightfully yours.

DEALING WITH BIG-BOX RETAILERS' SECRET WEB SITES

You love shopping online. You enjoy the convenience of surfing from home, the office, or the coffee shop. You find what you want to buy and the price you want to pay. The Web site tells you that the item can be purchased online or at your local store and you drive to the store to buy it.

So, are you surprised to find that the price at the store is higher than what you saw on the same store's Web site? Of course you are. Are you also surprised to find that if you go to the in-store kiosk and surf their Web site to look at the item there, it shows the same higher in-store price, rather than the lower price you saw online at home? Of course you are.

So, here's another element of surprise: At least one big-box retailer has admitted to offering higher prices via a "secret Web site" from their in-store kiosk Web site than the prices for the same items available on the Web to anyone outside the stores.

In other words, your reward for driving to their store and giving them your business is to pay higher prices because you drove to their store to give them your business. Is there a way to corner these guys and their tricks? Of course.

CULPRIT: Big-box retailer full of . . .

PROBLEM: . . . profit-producing pricing tricks

Any time you are shopping for an item online that you intend to pick up at a local store, make sure you print out and save a copy of the Web page you are looking at, and make sure it includes the price.

Now take this printout with you to the store when you go to purchase the item. That way, if the in-store price or the price on their in-store kiosk is higher, you can show them the printout and demand that they match their own Web site's price. But let's take this even further.

Most big-box stores offer price matching against their competitors' best prices. At many stores, their price-matching guarantee will not only match but beat the competitor's price, sometimes by as much as 10%. So why not use your cell phone with Internet access to find better prices for the same item on competitors' Web sites while you're standing there in the store? Then, pay for the item and walk over to customer service for your price-matching refund that has now enabled you to buy the item for less than you would have paid at either store.

DEALING WITH RETAIL OUTLETS THAT DEMAND YOU SHOW YOUR RECEIPT AT THE DOOR

We've all made this purchase at some point in our lives: We pay for our goods and then we're cherry picked by a receipt checker to make sure all the items in our basket match the receipt. This is not only unnerving, it's fairly inconvenient. This is the last thing we're interested in at the conclusion of our shopping experience. The nerve of these people, eh? Don't they have better things to do, like keeping the cart guy in line, talking to the security officer, or gossiping about their coworkers?

We're told that this inconvenience is for our own protection—but how so? What if you wanted to decline this protection because:

- It forces you to stand in yet another long line?
- It makes you feel like a criminal instead of a loyal customer?

A handful of shoppers around the country have found out that refusing to show your receipt could earn you a trip to the pen. You would at least have a good excuse for why you didn't make dinner on time.

According to *SmartMoney* magazine, retailers *cannot* require you to show your receipt. In fact, if you find this receipt-checking practice to be insulting and appalling, you can take matters into your own hands by avoiding the process altogether!

CULPRIT: Overly scrutinizing retailer

PROBLEM: Chewing into your precious time with "retail games" like receipt checking

BEST WAY TO WORK AROUND THIS ANNOYANCE: Treat "receipt-checking" like a game and challenge yourself to find new ways to avoid it. For example:

Make up a rule that receipt-checking is just for people who have bought huge cartloads of stuff and to avoid this insulting cherry-picking game, leave the cart behind after checking out, and fill up your hands and arms with all the stuff you just purchased.

Put the receipt where few will dare to pester you: in your mouth.

Whiz by the long line of carts and receipt checker as quickly as possible, keeping your eyes focused on the exit to "receipt-checking freedom."

"What if this doesn't work?" you ask. Pretend like the receipt checker doesn't exist—force them to gain your attention then greet them with a smile and a wet receipt. That ought to deter them from harassing you further!

WAKING UP FROM *THE MATRIX* AND STICKIN' IT TO RETAILERS ON "BLACK FRIDAY"

If you really want to stick it to the man, this section just might be the most important part of the book. You've probably seen *The Matrix*. Keanu Reeves' character—Neo a.k.a. "The One"—exists in an altered reality that's controlled by software programming—much like the controlled reality we live in today. *The Matrix* is all about social manipulation and so are the leading puppets of the world's governments, corporations, and more.

What if I told you that most of what we've learned about life was one fat, overarching, unrealistic *lie*? If you recall your childhood, you were pitched a fantasy about a guy in a red suit who loves visiting random homes, gobbling up milk and cookies, and leaving presents under a tree based on your behavior over the year. He only visits during one night and somehow manages to reach the entire world with a few overworked, underpaid, flying reindeer. I bet you actually believed that they could fly, didn't you? It's okay—it's *our* secret! I *promise* not to tell!

How did we fall for this nonsense? Our parents, of course, because we believed everything they told us. How dare question our parents, right? Unfortunately, they were simply repeating what *they* were taught as children, because they simply didn't know any better! As you got older, your parents probably sat you down one day (when you were about fourteen) to have a "serious talk" with you. They had to "come clean" about that jolly guy you always knew as Santa. They explained that they were sorry for misleading you, proceeding to console and comfort you with the same milk and cookies they pretended to leave around every Christmas for him, along with a box of Kleenex to clear up the remaining confusion you felt within. Oh, the trauma!

Or, if you were like me, you figured out at a very early age that good ol' Santa was a figment of our imagination (or better yet, a "brand" to drive sales). Regardless of how you arrived at this conclusion, many people today still choose to pass on this horrific "tale" to their offspring. Like a broadcast network, we subconsciously repeat "tradition" in the name of a last-minute race to boost the year end "numbers" of Macy's, Best Buy, Radio Shack, Kmart, Target, Saks, and whatever other retailer you can think of who benefits from this nonsense! Why?

We've been suckered for years with an endless supply of candy to maintain the "Santa brand" so that we'll continue dumping our wallets and the piggy banks of our children to "shop till we drop." Without fail, we're magically commanded each year by a bombardment of TV, radio, and Internet ads to spend, spend, and spend at the end of the year:

"Come get yourself a good deal!"

"You're not really saving a bundle, but we want you to think so!"

"Don't be a bad parent—buy new stuff for your kids!"

"Keep Santa's mission alive and fill your tree with presents!"

I don't know about you, but I'm feeling pretty nauseous. "Santa" is simply a decoy for corporations to make money during "manufactured holidays"—plain and simple. It's a creative marketing approach to get you and everyone in

your family to buy new products for each other—all in the name of "giving."

How much longer will we continue allowing the Krispy Kreme addicts in suits to lead us around on *their* leash? Shouldn't we be tired of eating the same ol' dog food about now? The ingredients haven't changed in well over a century and they have no plans on altering the taste anytime soon—so long as you continue to eat it! That's what they enjoy more than anything. They understand very well that you're hooked like a fish on their rod—that is until you wake up and close your wallet.

So, how do you show these guys "where to shove it" with a WIDE smile?

CULPRIT: People who manipulate the world each year to buy more stuff

PROBLEM: Not realizing that we're actually on their leash

BOOTING THEM OUT OF OUR WALLETS, PURSES, AND MINDS: Here are a few ways to put these guys on permanent notice:

Stop believing everything you're told—Research the origins of "Santa" and all the other crap you've learned about in life.

Stop running out and buying more crap for people—Chances are, they don't deserve it anyway.

Stop the perpetual cycle of wasteful spending—Give the circulars to your dog during playtime.

Ban yourself from shopping during this time of year—Slap yourself silly each time you're tempted to break this rule.

Call up the retailers and tell them their gig is up— You're SO on to their clever tricks.

Be honest with your children—It will prevent them from lying to their children in the future.

In addition, there are a lot of resources on the Internet that cover the history of ol' Saint Nick and the awesome role he plays for retailers. You might also be interested in the realistic viewpoints of these folks:

- Peter Schiff
- Ron Paul
- Tom Cryer
- Alex Jones

Knowledge is power. Filter the darkness to discover the light. Oh, and have plenty of tissue. The truth is hard, and it's always sobering.

DEMANDING BETTER SERVICE FROM COMPANIES WITH HORRIBLE PHONE SUPPORT

You're at your wits' end as a customer of a company with horrible phone support. You've tried everything from threatening to find the agent and feed them a week's supply of McDonald's to bribing them with fresh cookies just to be better served as a customer. Unfortunately, nothing has worked and your head is ready to explode in anger.

Well, it's time to get tough and show these guys you mean business.

CULPRIT: A lack of quality phone support

PROBLEM: Your mounting frustration with it

CATCHING THEM IN THE ACT (AND GETTING AWAY WITH IT, TOO): First, go to Radio Shack and have them show you how to record phone calls. You can record calls to a tape recorder, digital recorder, or right onto your computer hard drive. Now, when you call customer service, you're going to record *their* calls, just like they always record *yours*.

But is that legal? It is if you take this tip from customer-service guru Ron Burley, author of the book *Unscrewed*:

At the beginning of the call, ask for the representative's name, employee number, direct line, and call-center location.

Now follow Ron's script to legally inform the customer service rep that you may be recording the call:

You: *Boy, I sound just like you guys.* [*Chuckle. Then state clearly:*]This call may be recorded for training purposes. [Little laugh.]*Maybe you could put in a good word for me?*

Representative: [*Laughs*] Sure.

You: [*Laugh*] *Thanks. Anyway, here's what's going on with me today . . .*

And as Ron Burley explains, "He's been informed, and therefore I am within my rights to record the conversation. It's not my problem that the customer service representative might not have taken my statement seriously."

BONUS! Tired of sitting and waiting while on hold? Then try this trick next time you call:

While pushing your way through all the choices offered by their voice mail prompts, choose the option for "Spanish" any time it's offered. Why? Experience shows that the operators are usually bilingual and the wait times are usually much shorter. And if you don't speak Spanish and they call you on it? Just play dumb and say you must have hit the wrong number by mistake.

THE UNPROFESSIONAL TRUCK DRIVER AND YOU: DON'T BE BULLIED

The highways and byways of our cities are filled with all sorts of vehicles and people. There are people who take driving seriously and others who couldn't care less. I even think some people drive for the sake of pissing other people off. I suppose we all have our way of preparing for the morning drive, eh? There are also people who simply do not deserve to be on the road. Where did they learn to drive anyway?

Well, enough about those four-wheeling, freewheeling cousins of ours on the roads. Let's talk about our big brother: the truck driver. He's big, sometimes mean, and is always intimidating to others. We fear the sight of him as he cruises alongside us, and we whimper like a dog that's afraid of thunder.

Truck drivers know the attention they command on the road. Most of them are very courteous and professional about this fact. Unfortunately, there are a few goofballs who are truly lazy, selfish, and just plain stupid. These animals speed like heaven is departing tomorrow. These heartless road warriors give the rest of their brothers a very bad name.

Well, it's time to show these bullies that four-wheelers can kick some eighteen-wheeling, fifth-wheel-pulling, 80,000-pound-hauling tail!

CULPRIT: Unprofessional trucker driver

PROBLEM: He's riding your bumper like a three-legged horse.

FANTASY PAYBACK: Give the bunny rabbit a shock of his life by first giving him "the finger" and then hurling a gallon of paint toward his windshield with pinpoint accuracy. High-five yourself or the passenger(s) in the car, then take the next exit and proceed to disappear like a ghost in the night.

THE GROWN-UP THING TO DO: Reduce your speed by 5 to 10 miles per hour in front of the truck driver, and then smile in your rearview mirror. He'll be unhappy that you forced him to downshift on such a tight deadline!

RUNNING CIRCLES AROUND COMPANIES THAT WON'T LET YOU CANCEL YOUR SERVICE

Thanks to the Web site Consumerist.com, it's easier to understand why it's almost impossible to cancel your account when you call customer service. "How could it be impossible to cancel an account?" you ask. Well, consider these experiences from Consumerist.com:

- You call to cancel your account, but a new bill keeps showing up every month.
- You call to cancel again, but you still keep getting the bill.
- You call to cancel yet again, but again, the account is not canceled.

Well, there's a simple explanation for the runaround—companies exist to make money, but it *costs* them money to provide customer service. What company wants to *pay* money to take a call from you when you're just calling to say you want to cancel your account? They're not interested in cancellations! They want more dinero! More pesos! More gold shillings!

After all, from the company's perspective, what you're offering them in this call is a raw deal! The truth is that, back at the call center, the people who answer the phone and who do a horrible job of answering your questions work on a—gasp—quota system. In fact, two of the most important quotas are:

↳ How many cancellation calls can you, the customer

service rep, deflect?

⮡ How many potential customers can you convince *not* to cancel?

For those of us who have never worked in a call center, this may seem trivial and aggravating, but for the poorly trained and poorly paid people who take these jobs, letting you cancel your account could actually cost them their jobs.

So when you call and cancel, and then call again and cancel, and call again and cancel, it never takes effect because the person you talk with at the call center never enters it into the computer out of self-protection. Who would have thought? They're saving their raw bacon from being tossed into the fire!

So, is there anything you can do about this?

CULPRIT: Customer service agent working for XYZ Bully Corp

PROBLEM: Refusal to cancel service (without your knowledge)

RESOLVING THIS NIGHTMARE: Now that you understand why canceling an account by phone requires an act of Congress, try canceling your account online instead!

ADDRESSING COMPANIES WITH CRAPPY CUSTOMER SERVICE

You're probably scratching your head and trying to figure out the context of "crappy customer service"—that's fine. However, if you do business with Dell, Verizon, AT&T, or some similar company, you're already well-acclimated with "crappy customer service."

When you're stuck in the middle of a customer service nightmare that requires lots of calls and time on your part, but never brings any resolution on the company's part, here's how you can flip the coin in your favor while minimizing the hassle for yourself.

CULPRIT: Company's lack of accountability

PROBLEM: A customer-service nightmare

THE BEST WAY TO END IT: Let your credit-card company handle the burden, so it becomes *their* problem, instead of *yours*.

Here's a case study in how this works: Let's say you have a problem with a company and they refuse to allow you to return an item that you don't need. You call and they refuse to give you an RMA so you can return the item. Next, you ask to speak to a supervisor. You're put on hold for an hour and finally the call is disconnected.

A week later, after you've cooled down, you call, and again they refuse to give you an RMA so you can return the item. Once again, you ask to speak to a supervisor and they put you through the usual crap: hold for an hour, only later to be disconnected.

A week later, in a state of disbelief, you try one more time. You call and they refuse to give you an RMA so you can return the item. For a third time, you summon the help of a supervisor. Yes, you know what happens next. You've been put on hold for so long that you've missed a few birthdays. The least they can do is offer you one cake, right? Not so. Once again, they've disconnected you for reasons you can't even understand.

Now that you've had enough of being treated like a second-class citizen, the next call should be to your credit-card company. Explain your experience, including the three one-hour calls on hold, to the customer service representative, then request that they remove the charge from your bill, since the company refused to deal with you in a responsible way.

A few weeks later, a letter will arrive from your credit-card company with instructions on how you should return the part or product.

BOTTOM LINE: If you have the discipline to pay off your credit card every month, it's a great idea to charge everything you can, so that if there's a problem you can make it the credit-card company's problem, and not yours.

BONUS! A lot of credit cards come with a free extended warranty, even though they never really promote it after you actually apply for the card. So if you own a product that stops working after the manufacturer's warranty has ended, check with your credit-card company to see if the card you bought the item with has an extended warranty program that will cover your loss.

SOCKING IT TO COMPANIES THAT REQUIRE YOU SIGN A "MANDATORY BINDING ARBITRATION" CLAUSE (PART ONE)

Somewhere in the small print (which you'll need a magnifying lens and expensive lawyer to read), many contracts you sign today (without reading) state that if there's a dispute between you and the company, you agree to settle the dispute using "mandatory binding arbitration."

What's that, you say? Let's dissect it word by word:

Mandatory—"Sorry, pal, you have no choice but to accept our agreement."

Binding—"You're stuck to us like glue and have no say in the final outcome of the arbitration process."

Arbitration—You and company agree on a qualified and unbiased third person to help you determine a fair outcome to the dispute.

Unfortunately, as *BusinessWeek* magazine reports, this is not how "mandatory binding arbitration" often works. Instead, here's how *BusinessWeek* sums up the process:

"What if a judge solicited cases from big corporations by offering them a business-friendly venue in which to pursue consumers who are behind on their bills? What if the judge tried to make this pitch more appealing by teaming up with the corporations' outside lawyers? And what if the same corporations helped pay the judge's salary? It would, of course, amount to a conflict of interest and cast doubt on the fairness of proceedings before the judge.

"Yet that's essentially how one of the country's largest private arbitration firms operates. The National Arbitration Forum (NAF), a for-profit company based in Minneapolis, specializes in resolving claims by banks, credit-card companies, and major retailers that contend consumers owe them money. Often without knowing it, individuals agree in the fine print of their credit-card applications to arbitrate any disputes over bills rather than have the cases go to court. What consumers also don't know is that the NAF, which dominates credit-card arbitration, operates a system in which it is exceedingly difficult for individuals to prevail."

Here's the takeaway from *BusinessWeek*: It's a recipe for getting screwed. No painkillers or sedation will be provided. *BusinessWeek* further states:

"In March [2008], Dennis J. Herrera, San Francisco's city attorney, sued the firm in California state court, accusing it of churning out awards for creditors without sufficient justification. The lawsuit cites state records showing that NAF handled 33,933 collection arbitrations in California from January 2003, through March 2007. Of the 18,075 that weren't dropped by creditors, otherwise dismissed, or settled, consumers won just 30, or 0.2%, the suit alleges."

Well, now it's time to play ball according to your

rules—not theirs. How? You can start by reading the fine print in contracts and also knowing what to look for. Sure, it'll be pretty boring, but at least you'll have a clearer understanding of where you stand with a company before executing your game plan.

For example, the "Mandatory Binding Arbitration" clause may go by other names like "Dispute Resolution Mechanism" or another legal term. Don't confuse "Mandatory Binding Arbitration" with "Voluntary Arbitration." The big difference here is the difference between the words "voluntary" and "mandatory," because "voluntary" arbitration can be a great way to avoid the clogged court system and avoid a lawsuit, as long as both parties have the choice to participate or not.

Whenever you encounter a "Mandatory Binding Arbitration" clause, scratch the clause out of the contract and initial it, or tell the company that you are only authorized to agree to voluntary arbitration. Notice the language suggested here: Don't tell the company you *won't* sign an agreement if it includes a "Mandatory Binding Arbitration" clause, because they'll just try to change your mind. When you say you're not authorized to agree to "Mandatory Binding Arbitration" clause and you put this in writing (i.e., by e-mail), you have let them know your hands are tied, and that no matter how hard they try to convince you, you simply cannot agree.

SOCKING IT TO COMPANIES THAT REQUIRE YOU SIGN A "MANDATORY BINDING ARBITRATION" CLAUSE (PART TWO)

Now that you're more informed about "Mandatory Binding Arbitration," does it frighten you just a tiny bit? It should.

And if you're sufficiently frightened, you may want to start contacting your bank, brokerage firm, credit-card company, cell-phone company, cable company, car-loan company, and insurance company and asking them about their policy concerning "Mandatory Binding Arbitration."

And if you don't like what you hear? Tell them you want to "opt out" of their "Mandatory Binding Arbitration" clause. And if they tell you that you *can't* opt out? Tell them you will take your business elsewhere.

Meanwhile, if you are in a contract with an end date, like a cell-phone contract, you may need to wait until the current contract ends to fight this battle with the company or to switch to a different company where no "Mandatory Binding Arbitration" exists.

BONUS! You know all that annoying mail your bank and credit-card company and the cable company send you, in addition to your monthly bill? Sometimes, they will slip in a clause in one of those annoying mailers that will notify you that if you DON'T opt out of "Mandatory Binding Arbitration" by a certain date, that you will, by default, be agreeing to their "Mandatory Binding Arbitration" clause.

The lesson to learn here: Even after you notify all companies you do business with that you are opting out of "Mandatory Binding Arbitration," you will still have to review your status with all of these companies on a regular basis to make sure they have not somehow managed to opt you back in without your realizing it. How's that for being a "customer"?

SOCKING IT TO COMPANIES THAT REQUIRE YOU SIGN A "MANDATORY BINDING ARBITRATION" CLAUSE (PART THREE)

At the time of this writing, there is a bill in Congress called the "Arbitration Fairness Act" and if you go to http://action.citizen.org/campaign.jsp?campaign_KEY=13661, you can quickly and easily send your congressman or congresswoman an e-mail about why you support the bill, and why you think he or she should support it, too.

NO MORE COLD, CRAPPY FAST FOOD: HAVE IT FRESH, HOT, AND NOW!

Fast food is quick, convenient, and tasty. It's so easy to swing into a line at your favorite restaurant for a hot sandwich, crispy fries, and a cold drink to quench your thirst after a hard day. You notice a restaurant and decide that you'll have dinner there. You're anxious to order your food. The aroma radiating from the place is driving you insane. If you could eat air, you would, because it smells that good.

Now that you've ordered your food, what's next? It's time to eat, of course! Chomp! Pure delight! Unfortunately, you're not too happy. The fast-food experience has disappointed you. You feel duped, to the point of misery. Your entire day has been spoiled because of a bad fast-food experience. You're now ready to go home with your tail between your legs, because you feel it's not worth the effort to get your money's worth. Well, of course it is!

Here's how to show that freckle-faced, red-haired, phony-smiling little girl a lesson she'll *never* forget.

CULPRIT: Crappy fast food

PROBLEM: Stale food a rat wouldn't eat

PAYBACK: Go inside and ask to see the manager. Tell them that you were given cold food and that you demand compensation. Next, tear open the bag and dump the food on the floor. Proceed to jump up and down on the food, telling the manager how badly he and his employees suck. Then, to top it all off, tell him you'll *never* return to the establishment and leave in a huff! That will show the fast-food industry not to jerk the consumer's chain.

THE GROWN-UP THING TO DO: Kindly approach a cashier and ask for the manager. Proceed to tell them that your sandwich and fries are cold. Do not *ask* for a fresh sandwich and fries. Tell them—in a polite and friendly way—that you will wait. This is the *easiest* way to get a fresh, hot meal!

STANDING TOE-TO-TOE WITH YOUR LOCAL HOSPITAL (PART ONE)

Every time you hear someone from the American Medical Association or from Washington talk to the American people about how technology can be used to help make our health system more efficient, etch the following into your head from the *Washington Post* about the sad state of accuracy that exists when it comes to hospital billing today:

"Mistakes have become so prevalent that a niche industry has evolved to help patients decipher their bills. Pat Palmer, founder of Medical Billing Advocates of America, estimates that she finds **multiple errors in eight out of every ten hospital bills she reviews**." The same article goes on to say that "Medical Billing Advocates says it has found as much as $400,000 in errors when it examined the bills submitted to self-insured companies."

And from BankRate.com: "American hospitals are fleecing patients out of billions of dollars annually, and experts say that while some of the overcharges are honest errors, many are deliberate. That's because hospital bills are next to impossible for consumers to understand, which means hospitals can hide improper charges behind mysterious medical terminology and baffling codes."

If this doesn't make your blood boil, what else will? So how can you keep hospitals honest if you're the victim of a billing scam?

CULPRIT: Careless, deficient, and dishonest hospital

PROBLEM: Over-billing for sub-par health care

A SOLUTION TO THE MADNESS: Frankly, the game plan begins before you are ever admitted to a hospital:

STEP #1: Change your mind-set about your upcoming hospital stay.

Most people leave it in the hands of their doctor's office and hospital staff to handle all the details, but if money is important to you, you will take a proactive and aggressive consumer approach to this series of economic transactions, instead. In other words, assume that *everything* is negotiable and look for ways to save money and cut out ridiculous costs everywhere you can.

STEP #2: Start cutting here.

Sure, it would be nice to have your own room at the hospital, but do you really want it if it's coming out of your own pocket? With this question in mind, it's important to call your hospital's billing department and ask them what you will be charged for your hospital room, and it's equally important to ask them what is included with the room and what will incur extra charges.

And don't be shy about asking for lots of details. Demand them. In fact, you should be quite pleasant and up front with the hospital staff about why you are asking, explaining that you're not trying to be a shrew but that you're terrified of facing a bill at the end of the hospitalization that you cannot afford to pay, so you are trying to cut out every unnecessary cost that you can. This approach should win you a friend and a cost-cutting partner.

So what kinds of things might you be able to cut out of your hospital bill? Here's an example that may amuse and horrify you:

- Ask if you will be charged for the box of tissues in your room.
- Then ask how much the hospital charges for that box of tissues.

After you recover from shock, ask your new friend at the hospital to note in your account that you will not need that box of tissues, as you will be bringing your own.

STEP #3: Plan your stay with your doctor's office.

Your doctor's staff is another set of people to befriend in your effort to save. Here is the info you want to get from them:

⮑ Estimate of the cost of treatment. You will want to run this figure past your insurance company to compare with their payout.

⮑ Knowing your doctor's estimated fee and insurance company's payout in advance may enable you to negotiate on your doctor's fee to significantly reduce your own copay.

⮑ Names of other doctors (surgeons, anesthesiologist, radiologist, pathologist, etc.) who will be involved in your treatment. Once you have this info, you will want to confirm that they are in your insurance network and also check with their offices about estimated fees.

Here's a crazy one: Ask your doctor if you can bring your own prescription drugs from home so you can avoid paying crazy hospital prices for drugs you already own. Review the section of your policy called "exceptions and exclusions" with your doctor's office to determine ahead of time what might not be covered and discuss any relevant "exceptions and exclusions" with your doctor's staff to avoid any unnecessary or redundant testing or procedures that might not be covered by your insurance plan.

STEP #4: Question *everything* on your hospital bill.

Before continuing, a few points should be made:

⮑ Honest human error is *acceptable* and *forgivable*, but you still want to catch it so you don't have to pay for it.

⮥ What is *unacceptable* and *unforgivable* are billing and administrative practices that are deliberately deceptive or downright dishonest.

Some of the most common hospital-billing errors (you be the judge of how deliberate and/or dishonest may be):

⮥ Duplicate billing for the same service. This is not as easy to catch as it may sound because duplicate billing may be spread out over multiple bills.

⮥ Billing for more days than the actual stay. Again, this is easy to overlook if you or your loved one has spent a lot of time in the hospital.

ALSO:

⮥ Make sure you aren't being charged for your discharge day, because most hospitals only charge for the admission but not the day you leave.

⮥ Over-billing for operating-room time is common, but you can make sure you aren't paying for more time than actually used by comparing the time you're billed for against the anesthesiologist's records.

⮥ Expensive work or tests that were canceled but still show up on your bill anyway.

⮥ Sneaky "up-coding" is when the hospital gives you a generic drug but charges you more for the brand-name drug.

⮥ Demand more detail rather than accepting charges for "lab fees" or "miscellaneous fees" at face value.

Why? Because these broad categories are great places to hide questionable charges, so it's essential that you get full details to confirm that charges are legit. If the billing department refuses to provide this level of detail, send an appeal in writing to the hospital administrator or patient ombudsman.

STEP #5: Understand the full consequences of incorrect hospital billing.

Yes, it will cost you more out of pocket now, but if you have an extended illness or extended hospital stay, it could also cause you to reach the upper limit on your plan's lifetime benefit cap much faster than necessary. And then where would you go from there?

STANDING TOE-TO-TOE WITH YOUR LOCAL HOSPITAL (PART TWO)

In Part One, you learned how to cut out all the fat and malarkey from your hospital bill, and now that you've got it down to just the changes that are legitimate, there's one more lesson to learn: Your hospital bill is *highly* negotiable.

How? Here's the scoop.

CULPRIT: Greenback-addicted hospital

PROBLEM: Not knowing that your bill is negotiable

CUTTING MORE FAT FROM THE HOSPITAL BILL: In fact, just by asking you may be able to get your bill cut by 25 to 50 percent—seriously! Here's how to ask:

- Start by asking what Medicare would pay if you had coverage.
- Then offer to pay on the spot if you can reach a reasonable compromise on the bill.

But why will your hospital negotiate with you? Well, they're already negotiating with Medicare and insurance companies, so there's no reason why they shouldn't negotiate with you, too. So all you need is to know to ask. In fact, once you understand how the system *really* works, it becomes much easier to negotiate:

Generally speaking, Medicare pays based on the hospital's actual cost.

Big insurance companies are able to negotiate rates because of their size and clout.

The only people who pay full price are people who are uninsured or underinsured and, of course, people who haven't read this book.

INSURING YOURSELF AGAINST THE SHADY PRACTICES OF INSURANCE COMPANIES

Insurance. We either shudder or swallow the pill of necessity. You know how insurance works, right? The insurance companies have armies of people (called actuaries) who gather mountains of statistics. The actuaries crunch the numbers to come up with statistics about the risks involved with everything we do in life, and you probably already knew that the insurance game is all about beating the odds.

But did you realize that what I just described is just one part of the game? In addition to betting on how often X, Y, or Z will happen to you, your insurance company is *also* betting that:

- You will buy too much insurance and you won't review your coverage every year to find places where you can safely cut back (which is really your fault, not theirs).

- You won't read your policy and you won't *really* know what coverage you're *really* paying for (again, not really their fault . . . other than the fact that insurance documents are almost incomprehensible to your average consumer).

- When they pay a claim, you won't carefully review all the documents and catch all the "errors" they've made in their favor (their fault! their fault!).

꜀ When they decline a claim, you won't fight back to get the coverage you paid for (their fault! their fault! their fault!).

I know what you're asking yourself: "Does this really happen? Do insurance companies *really* try to cheat people out of collecting when they're entitled?"

You bet they do.

CULPRIT: Blood-sucking insurance company

PROBLEM: It's an insurance company!

WORKING AROUND THE INSURANCE INDUSTRY: In fact, even as I sit here writing this entry, this story has come across the news wire:

"A Los Angeles jury yesterday awarded a quadriplegic man $10 million in a bad faith case against Atlantic Mutual Insurance Company. The jury found that Atlantic Mutual acted despicably and with malice and oppression in wrongfully refusing to settle a personal injury case in 2002. . . ."

Let me be clear: I am not suggesting that you sue your insurance company every time they don't give you what you want, but I do want to make the point that it is illegal for insurance companies to sell you insurance coverage and then try to avoid paying out claims when there is a loss.

So how do you fight back against your insurance company when you think they're trying to stiff you? Here are some tips:

TIP #1: Don't get mad.

When it comes to health-insurance issues, getting mad will probably do more harm than good. Why? Precisely because your insurance doesn't care, and if you're the one who is sick, you may only make yourself sicker. And if you're *not* the one who's sick, your anger is still not going to help the sick person you are trying to care for.

Instead, you need to take a detached perspective and play the game the insurance company's way, even if you're sure they're trying to screw you. Because, in all honesty, you're probably right.

In fact, at the nonprofit Patient Advocate Foundation, 94% of the cases they see were initially denied benefits that were published benefits in the health plan. Or, as the head of Patient Advocate Foundation says, "Receiving a denial of benefits is not unusual—it is completely usual."

Still, even when you know you're right, the only way you can really stick it to them is to play the game better than they do so you make sure you win.

TIP #2: Learn how to play the game.

In case you haven't noticed, insurance companies are big, fat, bloated bureaucracies. The only way you can ever hope to win a battle against them is to play their big, fat, bloated bureaucracy games. And here's what you've got to do:

- Get a complete copy of your plan coverage, not the lame two-page summary that came in your employee handbook. You can probably get this policy info from your HR department.

- Next, compare the letter of denial you got from your insurance company against what is included and excluded from your coverage.

The truth is, you may *not* find info about your treatment, which has been denied, but what you will surely find is language that basically says that "excluded are all other treatments that are considered experimental and are not covered."

Now that you've compared your letter of denial to your actual policy, it's time to make an appointment to go see the person at your doctor's office who handles insurance billing, claims, and appeals.

Ask this person to get a letter for you from the doctor explaining, in writing, why the procedure was necessary. You will send this letter and your own letter to the insurance company. You can find a template for the letter you will write at www.BankRate.com.

If this initial appeal is denied, you can seek help from the Patient Advocate Foundation, and there is no charge for their services. It's also worth noting that the Patient Advocate Foundation has a 98% success rate.

TIP #3: If you think you have a great case, forget all the rules above.

I'm not a big fan of lawyers and lawsuits, especially those personal-injury attorneys that you see advertising on TV. Still, for the right case, they can come in handy, because if you have a great case, they'll do their work for you for no money down.

TIP #4: Go "All Oprah" to attract a great lawyer.

Seriously, if you want to get a good personal-injury lawyer to take on your case, you're going to have to present yourself as someone with a great story and a great case that's got the potential to make a lawyer big-time famous. Why is that important?

It's important because the personal-injury attorney doesn't really care about you and your sad-sack, sorry life; all he or she really cares about is using you to make big money, attract bigger cases, and to become famous.

So how can you use your unfortunate hospital story to get famous? It may not be as hard as you think, and to find out if you have what it takes, pick up a book called *Celebrity Branding You* by Nick Nanton, and study it well.

STAYING A STEP AHEAD OF YOUR AIRLINE (PART ONE)

The rules of the travel game have changed over the last few years. Today, you must be smarter, wiser, and more creative to get better deals and better service. Here's how to play the "airline game": If you've got to be somewhere on Thursday, try making plans to leave on Tuesday. That way, no matter *how many* delays you encounter, thanks to your airline, you will still get there in time for your meeting, romantic rendezvous, or whatever.

That being said, it also pays to be an aggressive traveler, which will help you secure a seat and much more.

Ready to stay one step ahead of your airline?

CULPRIT: The airline

PROBLEM: Fewer options and more expensive fares

SOLUTION: Be smarter than the average bear.

1. Don't check bags. If you do, it will be a lot harder for you to change flights if your flight is cancelled or delayed or running late or is low on toilet paper or anything else that could cause it to sit at the airport instead of taking you into the friendly skies.

2. Make sure your cell phone is fully charged. At the first sign of trouble, do two things simultaneously:

🔖 Jump in line

🔖 Use your cell to call the airline

While you wait an hour or two in line to get booked on another flight, you can also be negotiating with the folks at the call center to get rebooked over the phone. With any luck, one of these two strategies will work.

3. Make sure your laptop is fully charged, too. It's good to have an arsenal of tools (cell phone, laptop, etc.) charged and ready in the event you're faced with flight changes, cancellations, or a stray cat wandering onto a plane and leaving an unpleasant scent for your fellow seatmates.

4. Do the airline's job for them. Here are two advantages you have over airline personnel:

᭑ You've got lots of time on your hands as you stand and wait in line.

᭑ You have superior reasoning skills that you can put to work for you while you stand and wait in line.

5. Finally, here's what you should do with your extra time and reasoning skills:

᭑ Figure out where the nearest alternate airport is to you or the names of all alternate airports for your

destination city. When it's time for you to talk to an agent about your sad stuck-at-the-airport plight, you can suggest that you could fly out of Baltimore instead of D.C., or that you could fly into San Jose instead of San Francisco.

And here's the bottom line: Getting *close* to your destination and renting a car is always better than standing around an airport hoping you'll someday catch a flight that's going to exactly where you want to go.

To really walk a mile ahead of your airline, make a mental note of the following:

"According to Rule 240, you are required to put me on any other airline's flight that is going to the same destination."

To really win the battle using Rule 240, it's best to go to your airline's Web site and print out their "conditions of carriage" before heading to the airport. After all, it's hard for the airline to argue with what's written on their company Web site. But please note: Rule 240 will only help you if the delay is caused by the airline itself, but they're not bound by it if the problem is weather or war or other events or circumstances outside of their control.

STAYING A STEP AHEAD OF YOUR AIRLINE (PART TWO)

Oh, the pleasure of flight. Sure, it can be an adventure, but it's not always a perfect experience. You know the drill:

You're waiting at the airport for your flight to leave. Waiting, waiting, waiting. Finally, your airline announces that your flight is canceled or delayed because of bad weather.

Why is the problem always weather? Or, better yet, the inbound plane is being grounded due to a drunk pilot, mechanical failure, or some other event. Well, if it's bad weather, that's an act of nature, and it gets the airline off the hook. But is it *really* bad weather?

Or is it just a creative business tactic to avoid having to put you up for the night?

Again, it's all about staying a few steps ahead of your airline.

CULPRIT: The airline

PROBLEM: Pulling the wool over your eyes about "weather delays"

GETTING THE FACTS FOR YOURSELF ABOUT WEATHER DELAYS: Grab your mobile Web-enabled phone or laptop with Internet access.

Go to the Weather Channel's Web site (www. weather.com).

Bring up a map for current weather conditions that include your origin, your destination, and all the terrain in between.

See any bad weather there? If not, it's time to take your phone or laptop up to the desk to have a chat with the agent about your complimentary accommodations for the night. They'll be happy to see you—and be sure to smile while presenting the facts.

WRINGING BENEFITS FROM YOUR AIRLINE'S FREQUENT-FLIER PROGRAM

So you've been gathering those miles for years and now you want to *use* them?

Silly, silly you. If you want to use the miles during peak travel times like summer or around Christmas, you're going to have quite a challenge on your hands, since the airlines go out of their way to entice you to collect miles but also go out of their way to make it difficult for you to actually use them.

What's the point of "frequent flier" programs again?

CULPRIT: Stingy little frequent-flier-mile program

PROBLEM: Flying according to someone else's schedule

BEING SMARTER THAN THE LITTLE STINGY MEN WHO CONTROL "THE GAME": Plan *really far* out in advance.

Want to you use your miles to go a popular destination *next week*? Not happening. But, you *can* significantly increase the odds of finding free seats if you plan 331 days or 31 days out.

Why 331 and 31 days? I'm not sure anyone really knows, but this much *is* known: If you try to use your frequent flier miles more than 331 days out, you'll be told that rewards seats for those dates aren't available. If you want to go to a popular destination and don't book early (i.e., 331 days out), you're most likely going to be told that all the frequent-flier seats are already sold out. Thirty-one is also a useful number to keep in mind, because about a month before your desired travel date, the airline will start to have cancellations or even open up more seats for frequent fliers

Forget the Web. Use the phone instead! You'll almost never hear me tell you that sitting on hold waiting for a human is better than doing things yourself online, but in the case of using frequent-flier miles, making a call and paying a small extra fee to get the help of a smart human is definitely the way to go if you can't seem to find a way to nail your travel plans online on your own. Here's why:

↳ When you use your airline's Web site to research frequent-flier flights, it probably will *not* show you options that use their travel-partner airlines, too.

If you turn on the charm and befriend a good reservation agent, you will find that he or she will know some other tricks, like these, that can help you nail down your itinerary:

↳ Plan creatively using alternate routes or alternate connecting cities.

↳ Change your destination to a nearby city or airport that's less popular, but still gets you close to your ultimate destination.

↳ Figure out how to use "open jaw" itineraries to cobble together a final travel plan that still works for you. An "open jaw" ticket is one where you fly from A to B, get to C somehow other than flying, and then fly from C home to A.

↳ Book the trip for your second choice of dates or for dates you *don't* want, because you will (with any luck) be able to nail down the specific dates you *do* want at a later time.

↳ In fact, see the thirty-one-day rule mentioned earlier, but also keep trying to change your dates on a regular basis long before the thirty-one-day rule kicks in, if you can. Book your trip for dates that are *after* the dates when you actually want to go, then just show up at the airport and throw yourself at the mercy of the ticket agents there, and make sure you have a very good, very entertaining story to tell about why you're at the airport now instead of on the date you actually booked the flight.

BONUS! A Web site called Yapta (www.yapta.com) will let you track the availability of frequent-flier seats on your airline for your destination. It's also worth mentioning that Yapta's main claim to fame is that it's a free service that will track the purchase of your airline ticket even after you buy it and then help you get a refund if the price drops after you make your purchase.

AN INFORMED FLIER IS A HAPPY FLIER: BEING MORE CLEVER THAN YOUR FELLOW AIRLINE PASSENGERS

It's time for another trip to the airport. Only this time, you've come more prepared than the last. Gazing at the departures screen, you note that your flight is on time. That's always a relief, right? Wrong!

CULPRIT: Your airport's information screens

PROBLEM: Misleading travel information

STAYING ON TOP OF YOUR FLIGHT'S SCHEDULE: All that's needed is a cell phone and signing-up for a flight alert on your specified airline's Web site. Once you've asked to be alerted about any flight delays, schedule changes, or cancellations, you won't have to worry about faulty information displayed in the airport.

Here's the scenario once you've signed up for flight alert:

↳ Your phone rings or buzzes.

↳ It's a recorded call or text message from your airline notifying you that your flight is canceled or delayed. Pretty crazy? Not so much.

↳ Since you signed up for this alert on your phone, you know about the delay or cancellation before almost everyone else on the flight. What does this mean? Drum roll, please . . . It means you get to fly (excuse the pun) through the rebooking process quickly and hassle-free while all your fellow passengers are still sitting there thinking the flight is on time.

FINDING A DEAL AT A HOTEL (PART ONE)

"All hotel rooms look the same in the dark," says Tom Bodett, the Motel 6 spokesman.

Maybe so, but still, given a choice, I will take a Westin or a Radisson or a Ritz-Carlton over a Motel 6 any day. However, what I like *better* about Motel 6 is that they charge you for a clean, comfortable room and they *don't* nickel-and-dime you to death.

But at the fancier, higher-priced hotels, they're constantly trying to get more money out of your wallet before and after you check in. For instance, let's say you put some leftovers from dinner in the mini-bar fridge. Then, the next morning, you receive your bill and it includes a $20 charge for a bottle of wine. But you haven't checked out of the room yet and you didn't eat or drink anything from the mini-bar, so why would the hotel think you had a bottle of wine?

Here's the answer: At many hotels, there is now a sensor in the mini-bar fridge, in addition to a bunch of overpriced food and drink. So, if you open the fridge and move anything inside, it's highly likely that you will trigger an additional charge to your bill. Is this nuts or what? And if you think about it, this is a great way to make some additional revenue for the hotel.

After all, how carefully do most of us really look at our hotel bills, especially business travelers who just add the totals to their weekly expense accounts? So when staying at any hotel, it has become more and more important to look closely at your bill before checking out.

And what if your room has a mini-bar? Give it a body block as you first enter the room and hit it hard, to make sure *everything* in the fridge gets shifted around. That way, the sensor will register that you ate and drank everything in the fridge, which will tip the hotel off that there's been some kind of error.

STICK IT TO THE MAN • **115**

FINDING A DEAL AT A HOTEL (PART TWO)

At the risk of sounding like a shill for Motel 6 again, one other thing I really like about the chain is that you can make local calls for free, and there's no extra charge for using your long-distance service to make long-distance calls.

You certainly won't find such a generous policy for dialing out at many other hotel chains. In fact, if you're not careful, you can rack up some pretty hefty charges at a hotel without making very many calls at all. So here's how to stick it to the man when it comes to dialing out from your hotel room:

↳ Go to Accuconference.com and sign up for your own toll-free number. Signing up is free and getting this toll-free number will cost you just $2 per month.

And once you're at a hotel and want to make a call out:

↳ Log into your account on your computer or cell phone at www.AccuConference.com.

↳ Go into your AccuConference account and direct your own toll-free number to dial the number you want to call.

↳ Now dial your own toll-free number for free from your hotel phone, and your call will be sent to the number you want to call.

All calls you (or others) make to your toll-free number will be billed at about 6 cents per minute, which is dramatically less money than what your hotel would charge for an outgoing call.

AVOIDING THE PITFALLS OF TRAVEL WEB SITES

Here's the good news: They make it easier to find and compare prices.

And here's the bad news: When it comes to booking plane tickets, using a travel Web site will turn out to be a nightmare if you need to make changes to your ticket later on.

Here's why: If you book your flight through a travel Web site and then need to make a change, the odds are that your airline is going to make you go back to the travel Web site to make the change. This is going to cost you a bunch of wasted time, and it's probably also going to cost you some additional fees. With that in mind, here's how to use the power of travel Web sites, while avoiding the hassles and extra fees if you need to make a change:

Do your search on the big travel Web sites like Orbitz, Travelocity, and Expedia.

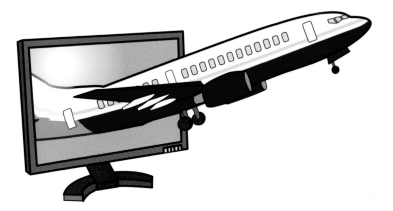

Compare the rates you find against a few deep-discount travel Web sites like Hotwire, TravelZoo, and Quickbook.

Now blow all these travel Web sites off and go directly to the airline or hotel Web sites to see if you can match or beat the rate there.

The advantage, of course, of making your reservation directly from the hotel or airline is that it will be easier for you to make changes later on.

But here's one exception. At the time of this writing, Orbitz will let you cancel a flight within twenty-four hours for only a $25 fee, which means that if you *think* you're going to make that trip and you find a great airfare, you can now afford to lock the airfare in knowing you will only pay a small penalty if you change your mind about the trip within the twenty-four-hour window.

BONUS! The biggest trap you can fall into when aggressively shopping for the best airfares and hotel rates online is to spend hours and hours searching and after all that time, still only saving $20 or $30. After all, your time is worth money, too, and you're a real sucker if you stay up all night looking for the best airfare and only have a $20 savings to show for it.

Thus, to make sure you don't end up sticking it to yourself when searching for great online travel rates, look at the clock when you start searching, write down the time, and give yourself an hour to look around. Then, at the end of that hour, lock in the best rates you've found so far, and go to bed and get some sleep!

SKIP THE LOCAL CAR MECHANIC: BE YOUR OWN FOR PENNIES ON THE DOLLAR

Some people are blessed with the "car-fixing" gene, and I wasn't one of them. Until recently, every time I've had car trouble, I get this "Oh, I'm screwed" feeling deep in my gut. Sound familiar? If so, here's how you can stick it to your local mechanic or auto shop: Don't take your car there.

Instead, go to a Web site called "JustAnswer," where for about $25 you can ask questions and engage in an online dialogue with a well-qualified mechanic for just about any make and model of car.

So when you're having car trouble, make your first stop this Web site (where you can also ask medical questions, legal questions, and home repair questions), where you may get all the info you need to make the repair yourself. Even if the repair is *not* something you can fix yourself, for about $25 this is still a great place to go for a knowledgeable yet inexpensive second opinion after your local mechanic has made a diagnosis.

NEGOTIATING YOUR WAY TO A BETTER DEAL AT THE GYM

I have a buddy who gets paid buckets of money to travel around the world teaching business executives how to negotiate. But here's the joke: One day at the gym, we were comparing notes on how much each of us was paying in monthly dues.

Do you need me to tell you the punch line for this joke? I'd rather tell you how to negotiate your own great deal, instead. You must remember this:

- It's only a gym.
- It's not the house of your dreams.
- It's not the car of your dreams.
- It's not the lover of your dreams.
- It's only a gym.
- And it's not even the *only* gym.

So go in with eyes wide open and know that they will try to screw you the same way a car dealer would. Fight back, and fight dirty. You know the gym you *really* want to join?

Don't go there first. Instead, go to a couple of nearby gyms that you really *don't* want to join. Go in and play hardball with them. Refuse to pay an initiation fee. Refuse to sign an annual contract. Demand towel service and spa service and "Reserved for You" stenciled onto one of the spin bikes.

And here's why I want you to go into these other gyms with all guns blazing: it will give you a chance to practice being a hard-ass, and to practice making unreasonable demands. After some of your demands are met and you get them in writing, you can use the offers you got from the less-desirable gyms to negotiate a better deal from the gym where you *do* want to go.

Negotiate with a friend. You know what a gym salesperson hates more than losing a customer? That's right . . . losing *two* customers.

So take a friend with you when you go to negotiate, because you two can play "good cop/bad cop" with the salesperson and work him or her over negotiating for a money-saving "Buddy Plan." Meanwhile, dealing with two prospective new clients at once will make it harder for the salesperson to say no to any of your demands.

Drive a hard bargain during the slow season. So when is that? For most gyms, it's in July and August, while everyone's on vacation. And it's in December, also, while everyone's stuffing themselves with lots of holiday food instead of working out and joining gyms.

If you don't get what you want, walk out the door. Let the salesperson chase you. Continue negotiating while you have your car door open and the engine running. And if you still can't get what you want, drive away, call the gym the next day, find out when this salesperson is *not* working, go back then and try again with a different salesperson.

LIVING FOR FREE AT A MALL'S EXPENSE

Not that you're ever really going to do this, but it sure is fun to think about: An artist in Providence, Rhode Island, watched as a new mall was being built in his neighborhood. As he watched, he noticed there was a funny little space in one of the parking underground areas that was partially hidden from view and sure to go unused. So he figured out a way to use it.

Several years after the mall was finished, he snuck into the garage and built a cinderblock wall to seal off the unused space. As part of his wall, he included a utility door, and then he locked it. Presto! He had a free 750-square-foot apartment that he then furnished with a couch, TV, game console, china, and a dining area. He and his friends took turns living there in his secret underground parking-lot apartment for four years and, yes, I'm guessing that free parking was also part of the deal.

COLLEGE TEXTBOOKS: LEARNING WELL ON A "RAMEN NOODLES" BUDGET

Don't get me started on how ridiculous it is for people under twenty-five to take on a home mortgage's worth of debt just to get a college education. Instead, let's talk about how to reduce at least one major expense related to that college education: the price of textbooks. Here are some great tips on how to save a lot of money on textbooks from a Web site called ReduceCollegeCosts.com:

TIP #1: Seek out and buy International Editions.

Why? Because their content is almost always the same as the U.S. editions and while there may be cosmetic differences like a soft cover instead of a hard cover, the price is usually much, much lower. You can often find International Editions at www.abebooks.com.

TIP #2: Hit up your professor for a book loan.

Professors usually get sample copies of their textbooks. What do they do with them? They probably throw them on a shelf and forget about them. This means that if you go to the professor's office and ask if he or she has a spare copy you can borrow, there's a good chance you'll walk out with a free copy of the book to use for the duration of the term.

TIP #3: Use the "Search Inside" tool at Amazon.com.

This isn't going to work if the professor assigns you a *lot* of reading in a book, but if you're only going to be reading a few pages here and there, this free feature might save you a bundle.

TIP #4: View ads, get free textbooks.

So, how much are your eyeballs worth? At a Web site called FreeloadPress.com, they're at least worth the price of all your textbooks. Here's how the deal works:

- You register for the site for free.
- You fill out a survey before downloading each book for free.
- Each book has advertising inside.

Is it worth it? FreeloadPress estimates that the average college student pays $900 a year in textbooks, so it's up to you to decide.

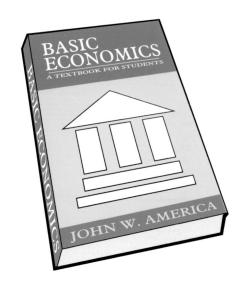

GREEDY BANKS AND CREATIVE WAYS TO BANK AN OUTCOME IN YOUR FAVOR (PART ONE)

Funny how we call our bank "*our*" bank, but if you look at the relationship objectively, things really work the other way around. For instance, when banks talk about *you*, they refer to *your* money as *their* assets.

So *whose* money is it, exactly? The question gets even foggier when you take a look at all the ways your bank finds to take your money away from you, because it seems like most commercial banks invent a slew of new and higher fees every year.

But I guess you can't really blame them. After all, banks have shareholders who want to make a profit on their investment. And to make that profit to make their shareholders happy, the bank has to find new and inventive ways to stick it to you, their customer.

But is there an alternative? You bet. It's called a credit union. They're not owned by shareholders, they're owned by the people who use the credit union to do their "banking." That's *you*.

Since there are no shareholders to please, credit unions usually have lower fees, lower interest rates for loans, and generally treat you much more like the respectable, decent human being that you are.

And why haven't you heard of them before? Let's see, credit unions are a better deal for consumers and when you use one you become a part owner. The fees are lower because it wouldn't make any sense for them to gouge their customers since their customers are also their owners.

And here's another reason their fees are often so much lower: They don't have to use those fees to pay for big national advertising campaigns to attract more customers that they can gouge. So, how much lower are credit-union fees? According to Bankrate.com, here's a sample of the savings that are just waiting for you:

- ⚡ Average bank fee for insufficient funds: $30
- ⚡ Average credit-union fee for insufficient funds: $20
- ⚡ Average bank fee for late credit-card payment: $39

- Average credit-union fee for late credit-card payment: $25
- Average bank fee for mortgage origination: $2,982
- Average credit-union fee for mortgage origination: $1,500

So how you do join a credit union?

Credit unions are funny things because to join one you have to fit into their specific "field of membership." A "field of membership" is a group of people who all live in the same place or work at the same company or belong to the same group or go to the same church.

So which "field of membership" do you belong to? To find out, go to www.FindaCreditUnion.com or the Credit Union National Association (CUNA) at www.CUNA.org.

GREEDY BANKS AND CREATIVE WAYS TO BANK AN OUTCOME IN YOUR FAVOR (PART TWO)

Here's a sneaky little trick your bank may be waiting to pull on you: without asking or telling you, they give you a free "service" called "courtesy overdraft." But there's nothing courteous about it, because it's actually designed to screw you.

Here's how it works: The bank sets up your account to automatically "lend" you money in case you ever write a check or use your ATM or debit card to use more money than you actually have in your account. This sounds sweet, right?

That's because I haven't mentioned that anytime you use this "courtesy" loan, it will also trigger a $10 to $50 fee to be drawn on your account, even if you're just overdrawn by a dollar or two. Meanwhile, here's where this "courtesy overdraft" becomes downright evil: At some banks, when you check your account balance online or at an ATM, they will pad or increase your account balance with their bounced-check protection limit, too, so that you happily spend away thinking you're spending *your* money, when in reality the bank has tricked you into spending *their* money and paying the associated fees.

So, what can you do to put an end to this heinous behavior? Call your bank and tell them you want to:

- Remove "courtesy overdraft" or bounced-check protection from your account.
- Add "traditional overdraft" protection to your account instead.

But what's the difference between the two forms of overdraft protection?

In the first type, "courtesy overdraft" or bounced-check protection, you are borrowing money from the bank and paying a hefty fee for the right to take advantage of this "courtesy" service. In the second type, traditional overdraft protection, you are using your own money from another account or a credit line to cover your overdrawn account.

But as you have already figured out, the bank would prefer that you borrow *their* money than *your* money, since they can charge you a whole lot more for it.

GREEDY BANKS AND CREATIVE WAYS TO BANK AN OUTCOME IN YOUR FAVOR (PART THREE)

Let's face it, your bank sucks. It sucks by charging you to use an out-of-network ATM. It sucks by charging you to go into the branch to talk to a human. It sucks because it has found a million other fees to charge you, too.

But here's one way you can stick it to your bank: Find a better place to keep your hard-earned cash by going to www.MoneyAisle.com and using their free service to find the best interest-rate nationwide for your savings.

How much more can you really earn? According to the *New York Times*, at MoneyAisle.com, you may be able to lock in interest rates for savings that are as much as a full percent higher than you would find at your local bank.

SHOWING YOUR CREDIT-CARD COMPANY HOW MUCH YOU LOVE THEM (PART ONE)

Let's be honest about your credit-card company—it is like a drug dealer; a heroin dealer, to be exact.

Too harsh? Too judgmental? Too unfair? Nope. It's a completely fair comparison.

Heroin dealers knowingly offer their customers a product that one can easily become addicted to, and the dealers will do anything to get you to try their goods because they know that once you're hooked, they've gained a customer for life.

Kind of sounds like credit-card companies, with their teaser rates and other special "introductory" offers, doesn't it? We all know how it works:

You sign up for the card with the *amazing* interest rate or the *free* airline ticket or with the 20,000 *free frequent-flier miles* or whatever.

And, for a while, you are diligent about paying the card off every month, or at least about making the minimum payment.

But then your credit-card company changes the rules on you in an effort to trick you into making a late payment that will trigger lots of additional fees and other consequences. Do I sound paranoid or conspiratorial? If you think so, then consider that MSNMoney.com agrees when they say, "Bank fees are more outrageous than ever." For example:

- In 1994, the average credit-card late fee was $12.55.
- In 2005, the average fee had grown to $34.42.
- In 1994, the average credit-card over-limit fee was $12.75.
- In 2005, the average fee had grown to $31.22.

And for those who will righteously say, "Well, if you paid your card off on time every month, you wouldn't be having these problems," consider that the "outrageousness" of the fees is not the amounts themselves but also the types of fees and the means by which banks are "tricking" their customers into triggering them.

Here are the kinds of tricks your credit-card company might pull on you:

Your bank or credit-card company may frequently change the mailing address where payment should be sent, which they know will certainly trip up many people who use snail mail to make payments.

By making the late-payment deadline in the middle

of the day, they ensure that even if your payment gets there by mail on the right day it may still be late if their mailroom doesn't deliver it by the appointed hour.

By making the due date on the weekend, they ensure that even if your payment arrives on-site on time, it doesn't get processed until Monday, which means late fees for you.

By making the grace period or payment due date so close to the date they mail the statement, that you'd almost have to mail your payment back the same day you receive the bill to avoid making a late payment.

So what can you do to "stick it" to your credit-card company, rather then letting them stick it to you?

CULPRIT: Deceiving credit-card company

PROBLEM: Missing your payment due date

A FEW TIPS TO AVOID THEIR "BILLING TRAPS":

TIP #1: Start reading your junk mail more carefully.

Do you ever get credit card offers in the mail? Yeah, me too. And lately, I've started reading them very closely.

Here's why: When I get a particularly great offer from Credit Card Company A, I pull out all my existing cards from Credit Card Company B and C and D and give them a call.

And here's what I say: "Hi, Credit Card Company B. I was just approved (not quite a lie since it says "You're Pre-Approved!" right on the envelope) by Credit Card Company A for a new card with only three percent interest and I'm hoping you can match that rate, so I can cut up that new card when I get it and keep using your card instead."

TIP #2: Know the right number to call.

Need to talk to someone at your credit card company? You could call the customer-service number on your bill if you want to wait on hold for three or four weeks. Or, you can look on the back of your card where it says "From outside the United States, call collect . . ." and then do as they say, and make a collect call.

Here's why this is important: When you call the regular customer-service number, they can afford to throw you in line to wait with all the other schlubs. But when you call collect and they think you're calling from overseas, your collect call may be costing them a lot of money, so they answer right away.

TIP #3: Be polite and persistent.

Here's the thing you need to know whenever calling customer service: When someone says "no" to your request, what it *really* means is "I don't have the authority to do that, but maybe my boss does." So don't ever accept "no" as meaning "no"; instead, just assume "no" means you need to be sent to someone further up the line.

TIP #4: Learn to use customer-service lingo.

Whenever you receive a "no," just keep requesting that the customer-service rep "escalate" you to the next level. When you finally hit a brick wall, it's time to use this magic phrase: *"I need to speak with a 'retention specialist,' please."*

TIP #5: Aggressively search for ways to stop using credit cards.

For instance, when you go to buy big-ticket items like a big-screen TV or computer, seek out stores that will let you buy the item interest-free with no payments due for twelve, eighteen, or twenty-four months. Then divide the total due on the purchase by the number of months you have to pay it off. Send in a payment for that much every month to 1) safely avoid paying any interest and 2) also avoid jacking up the balance of credit cards with the purchase.

SHOWING YOUR CREDIT-CARD COMPANY HOW MUCH YOU LOVE THEM (PART TWO)

Here's one way your credit-card company *just loves* to stick it to you:

They tell you that you have to make a minimum payment on your card every month.

Then you pay it, thinking that someday, oh someday, you'll actually pay the card off.

But the truth is, if all you ever pay is the minimum payment then you probably won't *ever* pay it off.

Here's why: Let's say your minimum payment for your card is 4% and your balance is $5,000, with a minimum payment of $200. What happens is that you make your minimum payment of $200 this month and you never make another charge on the card. Next month, your balance is $4,850 because $150 went to pay down the card balance and $50 was used to pay interest. And now that your balance is lower, your minimum payment of 4% is a bit lower; so in this bill, the credit-card company asks you to pay a minimum payment of $194.

You're all excited to see that your minimum payment went down, but that's because you don't realize that as long as your minimum payment gets lower and lower, you will have to keep paying off the card longer and longer. In fact, at this rate, it will take you almost eleven years to pay off this card. And the longer it takes you to pay off the card, the more interest you are paying to the credit-card company. In this case, you would be paying $1,622.42 in interest.

However, here's how you can stick it to your credit-card company, instead of letting them stick it to you: Stop paying the minimum payment and instead, pay as much as you can every month. If you continued paying $200 every month, instead of making lower and lower minimum payments every month, you would pay this credit card off in two and a half years (that's almost nine years less!), and you would only pay $782.44 in interest. (That's a savings of $840.)

BUSTING THE CHOPS OF TELEMARKETERS

I've had a longtime love relationship with a Web site called JunkBusters (www.junkbusters.com) because the site has taught me many lessons in how to fight back against sleazy, slimy companies.

If you want to know how to stick it to telemarketers while also potentially making some money for yourself, here's all the info you need, compliments of JunkBusters. com (with a few edits by me).

Every time you get a call you consider junk, just ask the questions in the following script. If they answer no, you may be able to *sue them*. How, you might ask? The federal Telephone Consumer Protection Act allows consumers *to sue telemarketers for illegal calling*. Most actions are brought in *small-claims court* for $500. But the law gives you a ready-made defense, which few consumers are willing to go to the trouble of trying to overcome.

If the call violates a previous Do-Not-Call request, the law allows one free violation per year, so be sure to put your phone number on the National Do-Not-Call registry by visiting www.donotcall.gov or by calling 1-888-382-1222. Meanwhile, it appears easier to secure a judgment based on "technical violations," such as failure to provide a *written policy*.

If you're determined to litigate, spend $10 on a booklet called *So You Want to Sue a Telemarketer,* available from *Private Citizen, Inc.,* by calling 1–800-CUT-JUNK.

Here's your telemarketer-busting script:

- "Are you calling to *sell* something?" (or "Is this a telemarketing call?")

- "Could you tell me your full *name* please?" $

- "And a phone number, area code first?" $

- "What's the name of the organization you're calling for?" $

- "Does that organization keep a list of numbers it's been asked *not* to call?" $

- "I would like my number(*s*) put *on* that list. Can you take care of that now?" $

- "And does the company you work for also make telemarketing calls for any other organizations?" (*If they answer no, skip the next question.*)

- (*If yes*) "Can you make sure your company won't call me for *any* other organization?" $

You may need to ask to speak with a supervisor if they sound lost. When you're ready to let them off, you might close with, "Is it clear that I never want telemarketing calls from *anyone*?" and just say good-bye.

If you feel like making them pay, keep going:

- "Will your company keep my number on its do-not-call list for at least *ten* years?" $

- "And does your company have a *written policy* that says that on paper?" $

- "Can you send me a *copy* of it?" $

⮮ "What's your supervisor's first and last name?"

⮮ "What's your employer's business name, address, and main telephone number?"

⮮ "Are you calling for a *tax-exempt* nonprofit organization?"

⮮ "Is this call based on a *previously* established business relationship?"

Before hanging up, check you have all their answers written down, then say good-bye. Add the date and time to your record. (Is it between 8 AM and 9 PM? **$**)

And now it's time for JunkBuster's disclaimer:

Nothing here should be taken as legal advice.

If they answer "No" to any question ending in "**$**" you may be able to *sue* them for $500–$1500 under the Telephone Consumer Protection Act. If, however, the answer to either of the last two questions is "Yes," then the Act doesn't consider the call to be a solicitation, so it's not covered by many of its regulations. Also excluded are calls to *business numbers*. For more details, see our pages on federal *laws* and on how to reduce *telemarketing calls* and junk mail.

GAME OVER FOR THE MOST ANNOYING PITCHMEN ON THE INTERNET: SPAMMERS

In a perfect world, you could drive over to a spammer's house anytime you wanted and smack him with a stick. But you can't. And any revenge fantasies you have had about somehow fighting back against spammers aren't going to work, either.

For a while, anti-spam professionals dreamed of finding a way to "spam the spammers" with their own spam as a way to put them out of business, but the truth is, spammers know how to build walls around themselves so there's no way to reach them, touch them, or hurt them.

But, there is *one* way to hurt spammers and that's to make sure no one ever sees their spam. There's a company called CloudMark that makes this possible, and here's how it works:

When you become a CloudMark subscriber you join a community of 700 million other spam fighters that works sort of like Napster or other peer-to-peer online communities.

In a nutshell, whenever someone receives a spam they can hit a CloudMark button on their e-mail program to mark the e-mail as spam.

When enough CloudMark members mark the message as spam, it automatically disappears from the inboxes of the other 700 million members.

So even if you can't go whack the spammer with a stick, you can, at least, make sure you never have to see his damn spam (and also make sure 700 million other people won't see it, either). You can buy an annual subscription to Cloudmark for $39.99 at www.cloudmark.com.

THE MONEY BANDITS: PROTECTING YOURSELF FROM CREDIT-CARD AND IDENTITY THIEVES

Today we're no longer shocked to turn on the news and hear that another large company's database has been hacked and that they have lost millions of customers' credit-card data. But here's an easy fix, compliments of a Web site called "Blueprint for Financial Prosperity."

Every few months, call all your credit-card companies and tell them you lost your card. They will happily send you a new card, because they certainly want you to keep using it to shop, but the new card will have a new number, and the old card number will become unusable.

End result: The next time a company's database gets hacked, they may get your credit card number, but it's not going to do them any good.

BONUS! While you're on the phone with your credit card companies, ask them to drop your cash-advance limit to $0. That way, if someone does get your card or your card number, they can't use it to get their hands on your cash.

THE ART OF LAW AND STICKING IT TO THOSE WHO STICK IT TO OTHERS

How do you stick it to someone whose job is to stick it to everyone else? Start by considering this: Chances are you don't need your lawyer anymore.

If you think about it, most of the legal stuff that most of us need is stuff that lawyers do over and over again but still get to charge $200 to $500 an hour to do the old cut-and-paste again for you. So why pay your lawyer a huge hourly rate when there's a way to get your problem solved with the same basic paperwork that the last hundred people were able to successfully use.

The solution is a Web site called LegalZoom.com, which has also received favorable reviews from the *New York Times*, the *Wall Street Journal*, and many other highly reputable newspapers.

FINDING AN HONEST, HARDWORKING REALTOR (WHO WILL WORK FOR YOU)

How's this for an oxymoron: great Realtor.

The problem with this profession is that it attracts a lot of people who just want to get rich quick without working too hard. The truth is, there are some *great* Realtors out there (yes, Barbara and Vince, I'm talking about you). But they're so few and far between that you should assume that you will have to meet at least twenty of them who are seemingly intelligent (out of a pool of, say, another eighty who aren't seemingly intelligent at all) before you find even one who appears to be even marginally good.

Or, you could just do the following when selling your house and completely subvert the traditional "Realtor" game altogether:

CULPRIT: You, and your unsellable home

PROBLEM: Lazy Realtor

SOLUTION: Find a young, hungry Realtor who wants to make some good money doing practically nothing. Propose to this young, hungry Realtor that you will pay him or her the following:

FOR SALE

But I have nicer properties for you to look at!

- $500 to list your house on the Multiple Listing Service. This is the database of houses in your area that only other Realtors can use and if you're NOT listed in the MLS, other realtors won't know about your house and therefore won't show it. It should also be noted that today, thanks to the Internet, buyers can go online and see some limited info about each house on the MLS, which makes your $500 investment even more valuable.

- Pay him another $500 to review the paperwork once you sell the house yourself.

Voilà! For a thousand bucks you get to advertise your house in the single most important place possible without paying someone a bunch more money for throwing an occasional "open house," which you already know you could do better. You also get some help making sure you do all the paperwork right to complete the sale. And what are the savings for you? Depending on the sale price of your home, you could save thousands and thousands of dollars.

"SHOCK AND AWE" YOUR WAY AROUND THE LOCAL CAR DEALER (PART ONE)

If you want to win at the game of buying cars, you have to do *at least* one of two things:

- Learn to think like a car dealer.
- Give up and just go buy your next car on eBay.

CULPRIT: Sleazy car dealer

PROBLEM: You need to buy a car.

SOLUTION: eBay.com

Here's what you need to know about buying a car on eBay:

- You can do it all online.
- You can get a pretty good idea if the seller is a scumbag by looking at the seller's rating.

- You can use eBay to get a pretty good idea of what other people are paying for the same car.
- When you are buying a car on eBay, it's a lot harder for the seller to use sleazy carsalesman tactics on you then when you are sitting there in the dealership. (More on this in the next section.)

Additionally, here's why eBay is such a powerful tool:

ᴸ You can see what people are currently bidding for the same car you want to buy.

ᴸ You can also see sales info for the past ninety days for the same car on eBay.

ᴸ On eBay, you will find all this info for both new and used cars.

All of this adds up to a marketplace where you have far less of a chance of getting screwed than you do when you walk into your local dealer's showroom.

Meanwhile, you can also use all the info available to you on eBay to stick it to your local car dealer by forcing him to negotiate with you against all the great prices you can find for the same or similarly equipped cars on eBay. So go to eBay, do your research, and then waltz into your local car dealer with printouts and/or your laptop and force-feed the salesman the info you have and berate them into beating the price on every deal you found on eBay.

"SHOCK AND AWE" YOUR WAY AROUND THE LOCAL CAR DEALER (PART TWO)

Before we move on, let's get a better appreciation for how car dealers work to stack the deck against you. For instance, consider the car-salesman trick called "Four Squares." Here's how it works. To help "get you" the price you want for the car of your dreams, your trusty, faithful car salesman pulls out a sheet of paper with "four squares" printed on it and he then proceeds to put the following four numbers in the squares:

- Trade-in value
- Purchase price
- Down payment
- Monthly payment

But here's where things get tricky.

All negotiations for the car will happen on the front and even the back of this sheet, and the sheet will get rather messy. And messy is a good thing for the salesman, because it will only help to confuse and distract you. Why does this simple, non-threatening little piece of paper make it easy for the salesman to screw you?

First of all, the salesman fills out the "four squares" with really stupid, high numbers for the purchase price and down payment and monthly payment and a stupid low price for the trade-in that only a fool would agree to, but hey, sometimes a fool walks in and buys a car for those numbers without trying to negotiate at all.

When you scream in protest at how high the numbers are, the salesman uses the sheet to force you to focus on just *one* or *two* of the high numbers, even if you think *all* of the numbers are objectionable. In fact, the salesman might even fold the sheet in half while negotiating with you to remove the other "stupid high" numbers from your sight so you forget about them.

The end result, in many cases, is that the salesman will let you aggressively negotiate to a better position on *one* number, because the salesman knows you are leaving a ton of money on the table by forgetting to unfold the paper and negotiate up or down all the other numbers, too.

And now, with all this in mind, here are some tips on how to negotiate wisely. Don't ever let them keep you focused just on one number like monthly payments, because if all you look at are payments, you are completely overlooking the actual price you are paying for the car *and* the finance rate *and* the value of your trade-in.

Want to fight back against the "four-squares" technique? One way to do it is to use your own sheet of paper to keep track of the negotiations; that way, you can review your own work at any time and freely go back and look at all the past numbers that have been discussed. Always remember that more than anything else, the car salesman wants this deal to happen, and he wants it to happen so bad he can taste it, and the *last thing* he wants you to do is to "go home and think about it." So one of your strongest negotiating strategies is to keep the conversation focused on all four numbers and if you feel things aren't going your way, suddenly announce:

⚘ "I love the car, but I'm not sure I can come up with that much down payment right now. I'm going to go home now and crunch some numbers, and if I

see a way to do it or even get close, I will call you tomorrow."

↳ "I love the car, but I think I can get much better financing from my bank or credit union. So I'm going to go home now and call them in the morning and then come back to buy the car tomorrow."

↳ "I love the car, but I think I can get a lot more for my trade-in by selling it myself. So I'll do that and come back and buy the car once my trade-in is sold."

Can't you just feel a wave of fear and horror shoot through the car salesman's entire body?

Use these deal-busters to negotiate, and you'll be amazed at how quickly the numbers on your "Four Squares" sheet start to drop.

Bottom line: The only way you can win this game when you walk into a dealership is if you are armed with at least as much info as they are and you know how to use it.

But let's face it, you *always* have one magic tool at your disposal that they do *not*. That magic tool is your feet. Unlike the dealer, you can always get up and walk out the door. Remember, they know that you're free to walk at any time, too, but they're doing everything they can to make sure you forget.

"SHOCK AND AWE" YOUR WAY AROUND THE LOCAL CAR DEALER (PART THREE)

Why do car dealers (almost) always win? It's because they've got easy access to all the info while most car-buyers are totally in the dark. But it doesn't have to be that way. In fact, if you want to stick it to your local car dealer, you've got to make sure you start thinking like them, get easy access to all the info, and use it against them the same way they try to use it against you. So, where are you going to find info like that? Dude, it's called the Internet.

Furthermore, a lot of the info you need in order to win is free, if you only know where to look. So when you're getting ready to buy a car, make sure you visit these sites:

- eBay, of course (see previous section)
- Edmunds.com

- Kelley Blue Book (www.kbb.com) if you're buying a used car
- Eloan.com and your credit union, for info on car loans

Edmunds.com is particularly useful when shopping for a new car, because you can find all kinds of "insider" info there, like the actual invoice price for the car you want to buy plus an account of all factory incentives your dealer will get when they make a sale to you.

And here's a good tip for when you move on to your local dealer: When you go shopping, take a laptop with you. Most dealerships have free Wi-Fi, for customers in the service department who are waiting for cars to get fixed. This is great news for you, because it means that while you negotiate with the salesman, you can be doing price research online and number-crunching with *your* computer while the salesman does his number-crunching research on *his* computer.

Then, when he offers you some stupidly high price on the car of your dreams, you can confidently slap down his offer by telling him exactly why it's too high, and then turn your laptop around to show him the proof!

BONUS! Once the salesman sees that you're a smart and informed consumer, it will probably be easy to get him to agree to sell you a car for a fair profit over the sticker price, say $300. Here's how you might bring him to this price-fixing agreement:

HIM: Well, you know we can't just give the car away.

We've got to make a profit or we'll go out of business.

YOU: I completely agree! Of course you deserve to make a profit! So how about if you and I agree on how much that profit should be right now? How does $300 over your cost sound? If that works for you, when I find the car I want, it will be easy for us to take the sticker price, add the agreed-upon amount of profit, and then subtract out any factory incentives and that should give us the purchase price we both are agreeing right now will be fair.

BEATING THE PARKING TICKET (AND THE METER MAID)

Like Gandhi, it's best to approach situations in a nonviolent manner. I mention this because I would not ever suggest that you do as a couple in Philadelphia did, which is to beat up a meter maid in order to get out of a parking ticket. Instead, I suggest that you stick it to the meter maid and fight your parking ticket like this: Read the ticket very closely, because if you find even one error, then you can follow the instructions on the ticket or envelope to protest the ticket and have it dismissed.

PROBLEM: Parking tickets

SOLUTION: Read your ticket closely.

According to one traffic-ticket insider, about 25% of all tickets contain at least one wrong piece of information. So check the ticket to make sure the following info is correct:

- Day
- Date
- Time
- Address
- Your license plate number
- Description of your car
- Parking infraction

Demand to see the calibration records for the meter where you were parked. Did you ever think about how important it is for parking meters to keep time correctly? If they didn't keep time correctly, the city would end up *stealing* from all those who park. That's why every city has a law that requires that meters be tested or recalibrated on a regular basis.

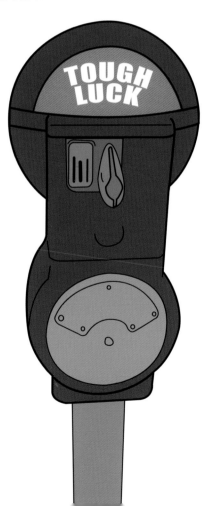

So when was the last time *your* meter got recalibrated? If it hasn't been tested within the prescribed time frame, then you should be able to protest the ticket and have it dismissed.

Rely on your cell phone, not just a paper bag. Here's the scenario: You finally find a parking space only to discover, after you throw all your quarters in, that it has a broken meter. Now what do you do? After all, it's the only space you could find and even if you *could* find another space, you no longer have any change. Here's a suggestion:

- Grab an old paper or plastic bag out of your car or trunk and throw it over the meter with a note explaining the problem.
- In addition to the paper bag, use your cell phone to take a picture of the broken meter, then use your phone to e-mail the photo to yourself or a friend.

Why? Because, you can use the time-and-date stamp on the e-mail to verify the time that you parked, and if you have a ticket, take another picture of the meter when you return to prove that even though the meter was broken you still only parked in the spot for the amount of time allowed by the meter itself.

OUTSMARTING THE COP WAITING TO CATCH YOU SPEEDING

First off, an obvious point: If you made it a habit *not* to speed, you could skip this section of the book. You also wouldn't have to worry all the time about your insurance costs going up. Your life, then, would be a lot less stressful, because you wouldn't always be watching your rearview mirror or be worrying about getting busted for speeding all the time.

However, if you are the type that just cannot resist pushing the speeding envelope, here's the best way to stick it to that cop who's hiding in the bushes: Learn to make yourself invisible to him. And here's how you're going to do it:

- Fix your burned-out tail light.

  Why? Because it provides a cop with good reason to notice you and pull you over.

- Lose the "Police Benevolent Association" sticker in your back window.

  Why? Because cops know there's only one reason you put it there, and that's because you're hoping it will help you get *out* of a speeding ticket. But isn't that almost like admitting that you're a habitual speeder?

🦶 Stick with the pack, especially if they're trucks.

If you're going to speed, speed with speeders—don't do it all alone. After all, if you're ahead of the pack and speeding, that means you stick out like a sore thumb. And if you're traveling with a pack of trucks that are all speeding, it's going to be a lot easier for the cop to focus on the trucks that are speeding by than on you.

STICK IT TO THE MAN • 163

GETTING DOWN TO BUSINESS WITH THE IRS (AND HAVING A "ONE UP," TOO)

Before you read this next section, here's the question you should ask yourself:

"Just how much do I want to stick it to the IRS, and how much do I want to stop paying taxes?"

CULPRIT: IRS

PROBLEM: You don't have the cash for your taxes.

SOLUTION: Do a runner.

A lot? If so, then here's what you need to do: Leave. Just leave for good. Why should you take that route? Well, the United States is the only developed country in the world that taxes its citizens while they are living overseas and that means that if you live in Paris or Tuscany or Dubai, you are going to be taxed twice—once by your homeland and again by your guest country.

So if you *really, really, really* never want to be bothered by the IRS again, here's what you're going to have to do:

Expatriate by giving up your U.S. citizenship.

You do this by renouncing "your U.S. citizenship outside the United States before a diplomatic or consular officer of the United States pursuant to paragraph (5) of section 349 of the Immigration and Nationality Act, provided there is a determination of loss of citizenship by the secretary of state, as reflected by your receipt of an approved Certificate of Loss of Nationality. . . ."

Or:

You are going to have to voluntarily "perform an act of expatriation with the specific and contemporaneous intention of giving up your U.S. citizenship, provided there is a determination of loss by the Secretary of State, as reflected by your receipt of an approved Certificate of Loss of Nationality. An act of expatriation is any act defined as a potentially expatriating act either by paragraph (1), (2), (3), or (4) of section 349(a) of the Immigration and Nationality Act or by any other Act of Congress defining expatriating acts."

The IRS says that "If you expatriate after June 3, 2004, until you file Form 8854 and notify the Department of State or the Department of Homeland Security of your expatriating act or termination of residency, your expatriation or termination of residency for immigration purposes will not relieve you of your obligation to file U.S. tax returns and report your worldwide income as a citizen or resident of the United States. For purposes of U.S. tax rules, the date of your expatriation or termination of residency will be the later of the date you notify the relevant agency of your expatriating act or termination of residency, or the date this form is filed in accordance with these instructions. For purposes of determining the date on which this form is filed, apply the rules of section 7502. Generally, this is the postmark date."

The IRS further warrants that "You are subject to taxation under section 877 if you are a former U.S. citizen or former LTR, and any one of the following applies to you:

"Your average annual net income tax liability for the five years ending before the date of your expatriation or termination of residency is more than the amount listed below:

- $127,000 if you expatriated in 2005
- $131,000 if you expatriated in 2006
- $136,000 if you expatriated in 2007

"This amount is subject to cost-of-living adjustments. The IRS will announce the amounts applicable to future years in annual revenue procedures that will be published in the Internal Revenue Bulletin. The Internal Revenue Bulletins can be accessed at: www.irs.gov/irb.

"Your net worth is $2 million or more on the date of your expatriation or termination of residency.

"You fail to certify on Form 8854 that you have complied with all of your U.S. federal tax obligations for the five years preceding the date of your expatriation or termination of residency."

THROWING 'EM OVERBOARD: SHAREHOLDERS FIGHT BACK AGAINST A "MEGA CORPORATION" AND ITS STUPID EXECUTIVES

In 2001, XO Communications—a multibillion-dollar telecommunications corporation—decided that it was time to run off with its shareholders' stake and into the loving and welcoming arms of renegade "Corporate Raider" Forstmann Little & Company. Until this point, XO was known for delivering world-class voice and data services to top corporations and small businesses throughout America. Unfortunately, the company quickly diminished its role as an "industry player" when word got out about its sinister, sneaky move that would effectively wipe out billions of dollars in shareholder equity.

So, what did the shareholders do? They certainly didn't sit idle watching the barrel of their money roll down the hallway to an entity known for stealing corporations away from its stakeholders. They didn't sit around with Kleenex in hand, waving farewell to their interests in XO. They didn't hide in a corner crying their eyes out. Oh, no, they revolted with knives, chains, whips, donkeys, mules, and everything they could possibly find to make themselves heard!

Using the Internet, they launched an unprecedented campaign that would make any "social network" today blush with envy. Here's how they did it.

CULPRIT: Back-stabbing corporation

PROBLEM: Refusal to notify its shareholders of its crooked plan

SOLUTION: Start a fire for the world to see. When news broke that XO would halt trading of their stock for an unspecified reason, investors—including myself— were on edge. Three weeks prior to this event, I had just invested a few hundred dollars in XO—my first-ever stock investment at the tender age of twenty-two. Three weeks later, I tripled my investment and was all smiles about my first rodeo in the stock market.

Bored and hungry for a new challenge, I was one day away from selling my proceeds to invest in a new company—simply to push the envelope of my limited knowledge in day trading. Of course, you can imagine my surprise when I heard the news from Wall Street that all trading was halted for the company. Palms sweaty, I made a visit to the XO MSN forum to discover plenty of chatter about this strange, secret event. Later that day, the bomb was dropped—XO announced its intent of agreeing to a leveraged buyout deal with Forstmann.

Ouch! The nerve of those selfish, secretive, bonbon-eating, no-fly-fishing executards!

Everyone was ready to do something. A community of hopeless and distraught investors was quickly forming, and many ideas for the next course of action were being discussed. While sifting through all the discussions on the forum, I was immediately attracted to the idea of launching a Web site to centralize a voice for the common XO shareholder. Instantly, I hopped on board as the site's designer and manager, while others handled the back-end stuff (for example, the database). Web sites do wonders to gather people. To centralize the voice of all of XO's shareholders, we planned and agreed upon the following:

- Acquired XOShareholders.com (see the archived pages at web.archive.org)
- Created a Web presence to accept stock data from each shareholder
- Announced the site via shareholder forums (MSN, etc.)
- Created timely information to inform shareholders
- Engaged the press about the site's launch

Within hours of our announcement of XOShareholders.com, shareholders, the media, and curious onlookers slammed our site with holdings information and news. I fielded shareholder calls from the Cayman Islands and other exotic regions, listening to their frustration and hopelessness. Our quick thinking—coupled with hard work—allowed us to develop one of the most successful shareholder grassroots campaigns in the history of the Internet—maybe even the world!

As news spread about XOShareholders.com via the *Washington Post* and other media, it would quickly amass some impressive data: 2,623 shareholders representing

23,394,959 million shares outstanding in the company. How's that for "centralizing" the voice of the common shareholder?

Frankly, the goal of establishing a voice for the common shareholder was realized beyond anyone's wildest imagination. It's only because of quick action, community, and the Internet that XO shareholders were successful in making their voices heard—even though, in the end, it wasn't enough to end the deal.

Should you find yourself in a similar position as a shareholder one day, remember this little-discussed story in grassroots success for inspiration and ideas.

"TRIMMING THE FAT" FROM YOUR RENT

It's lease renewal time and you *know* you've been paying too much rent. But you really like where you live and you really don't want to move. So what's the solution?

Rent-O-Meter, of course! This is a free Web site that will analyze all other rentals that are currently available in your neighborhood so that you can compare your current rent with what newcomers to your neighborhood are likely to pay now for a similar house or apartment. Here's how you can use Rent-O-Meter to get an edge on your landlord:

Call your local chamber of commerce, tell them you are the HR director for a company that is thinking of relocating to the area, and ask them if they have any info on seasonal fluctuations on rents in your community. For instance, they might tell you that rents traditionally are highest in the summer, and lowest in the dead of winter.

Ask the chamber if there is a local landlords' association in your community, then call them and ask them to confirm what you learned about seasonal rises and dips in rent.

While on the phone with your local landlord association and chamber of commerce, ask if they have any info from local business experts about three-month, six-month, twelve-month, and eighteen-month business and economic forecasts for your area.

Now armed with some useful info about your local economy and fluctuations in local rents, wait until local rents drop, and then contact your landlord and inform him that according to an unbiased Web site, "Rent-O-Meter," you are paying more rent than anyone in the neighborhood. Then explain that if he would be willing to lower the rent to something closer to what others in the neighborhood are paying now, that you'd be happy to sign a new lease for an additional year or two right on the spot.

But why would your landlord agree to this? Think about it. A landlord's worst nightmare is an empty house or apartment because:

- Once you leave, the apartment becomes a complete hassle for him.
- Once you leave, he has to spend a bunch of money cleaning and painting the place, and probably replacing the carpet and some of the appliances.
- Once you leave, he will probably lose at least a month of rent while the apartment is freshened up and before he is able to find a new tenant, and the loss of a full month's rent and all that cleaning and repairing probably adds up to a lot more money than the rent reduction you are asking for.

You have just shown your landlord that rents are going down, not up, but unlike you, he hasn't done his homework so he probably doesn't know the dip in rents is temporary and cyclical.

THE RIGHT WAY TO ADDRESS YOUR RUDE, LOUD, SLOPPY NEIGHBORS

Here's the right way to deal with your neighbors:

↳ Attempt to sit down with them and have a nice chat about whatever the perceived problem is—for instance, loud music late at night.

↳ If you think they are actually breaking a law, take a copy of the law or ordinance with you.

↳ It that doesn't help, warn your neighbor in writing that if they continue to break the law or ordinance that there will be consequences.

Still a problem? Then contact your city about the availability of free or low-cost mediation to resolve the problem.

Still a problem? It's time to call the police and if it's still a problem, you can sue in small claims court for nuisance provided you can show the following:

↳ Your neighbor is responsible, for instance, for excessive and disturbing noise.

↳ This noise leads to diminished enjoyment of your property by you and your family.

↳ You have made reasonable attempts to get your neighbor to correct the problem.

"THROWING A SHOE" AT YOUR LOCAL TAX COLLECTOR

Tax collectors. What comes to mind when you think of one? Never mind, keep those thoughts to yourself, because they're a bit too graphic for this book. Regardless of your opinion of this infamous profession, they can make or break you come tax time. According to Pete Sepp of the National Taxpayers Union, when it comes to property taxes, as many as 60% of all homes are assessed for too much, and about 33% of property-tax appeals succeed.

CULPRIT: The beloved tax collector

PROBLEM: Inflated home value

A STRATEGY FOR REDUCING YOUR PROPERTY TAXES: So where's the "silver lining" for you? The odds are in your favor that you could save a bundle every year simply by challenging the assessed value of your house.

You can start this challenge quite easily by contacting your local assessor and asking for a copy of your property card. This document shows the square footage of your house, number of bedrooms, and other relevant info, but if you find that any of the info is wrong, it may be easy for you to get your assessment changed without going through the appeal process.

If all the info in the document is correct, it might be worth going to Zillow.com to see how your house's value stacks up against comparable houses in your neighborhood. If you find here that other comparable houses in your neighborhood are paying lower taxes, you may have a very strong case for getting your house reassessed, and getting a reduction in your property taxes.

After all, what do you have to lose when it's free to appeal your tax bill in most communities or, at worst, may cost you a filing fee of $20 to $50? It's a small price to pay when looking at the bigger picture.

"SERVING THE PORK" TO YOUR CONGRESSPERSON

It's quite easy, really. Just get their list of donors—it's all public information. Then do a little digging to find out who the donors *really* are and where they *really* work and what they *really* stand for. Match up the donors with the legislation that your congressman or congresswoman has or hasn't passed. Odds are it won't look so good.

If you want a head start on this process, just go back and look at what your congressman's or congresswoman's last opponent said about him or her. Of course the opponent couldn't spill *all* the dirt they found during the last election because then too much dirt would have come out about him or her, too.

Think this is over the top? Think again! Consider the following story from the Web site CapitalHillBlue.com, "How to Buy a Senator . . . or a President" by news reporter Doug Thompson. He writes about how lobbyists can sway the opinions of Congress. Thompson ran the Political Programs Division of the National Association of Realtors, the largest trade association in the country, in 1987. He describes the scene as such:

"One afternoon, Steve Driesler, Senior Vice President for Government Affairs, walked into my office. 'We've got a problem,' he said. 'A member of the House Ways and Means Committee told one of our lobbyists today that mortgage interest deductibility in on the table.'

"*On the table* meant the committee was considering reducing or even eliminating the ability of American homeowners to deduct the interest on their mortgages on their income taxes. Mortgage interest deductibility is, and continues to be, a bread and butter issue for the real estate industry.

'Don't worry,' I told Driesler. 'I'll take care of it.'"

Thompson and his team put together a series of drive time radio ads to run over the next two weeks during morning and evening drive time, with a toll-free 800 number that would connect callers to their congressman.

After three days, Illinois Congressman Dan Rostenkowski, then chairman of the Ways and Means Committee, dropped the bill.

In Thompson's words: "It took just three days and $2.2 million to force Rostenkowski, then one of the most powerful members of Congress, to back down. The Realtors got their way because we had the largest political action committee (PAC) in town and we had no hesitation on spending money to exercise clout."

THE CARTEL KNOWN AS OPEC

Sometimes, when we desire to stick it to the man, we go at it alone. And sometimes, when we desire to stick it to the man, we have to band together.

And when it comes to standing up against the greedy suits that run OPEC and big oil, our only hope, says Jayanta Sen, a University of Chicago–trained economist who teaches at Nevada State College, is to make our own cartel that's even more powerful than OPEC. Imagine that!

OPEC, of course, stands for Organization of Petroleum *Exporting* Countries, so how about if we create a cartel called OPIC, the Organization of Petroleum *Importing* Countries? As part of this cartel, we could include the United States, Japan, Germany, China, India, France, South Korea, and China. The idea here is simple, as Jayanta Sen explains:

> "In the international oil market, the producers are cartelized, whereas the buyers are fragmented. As standard economic analysis suggests, this results in a greater share of the surplus for the producers. The cost of exploration plus production for a barrel of oil to the producers is approximately $14, whereas the recent price is $65."

BOTTOM LINE: Sen suggests that OPEC has been able to dominate and manipulate us through the price of oil precisely because they are a large organized group of *sellers* with a fairly unified voice.

But what if we became an even larger organized group of *buyers* with a fairly unified voice? Sen points out that in 2004, the world's ten largest oil importers imported about 32.6 million barrels per day. And what a coincidence! That's almost exactly what OPEC produced that same year.

The point is that while today we certainly need OPEC's oil or our economy could collapse, it's also clear that OPEC needs us to buy that oil, or their economies could collapse. By organizing, we would gain negotiating power we never had before and that's one way we, as a group, can stick it to OPEC.

BEING SMARTER THAN YOUR BOSS (WHILE SMILING YOUR WAY TO THE BANK)

"Impossible!" you say. "How can I stick it to my boss when he or she's got all the power?"

Before we go on, let's kill that notion about all your boss's power by talking about his or her greatest fear. He or she is terrified that:

- You'll walk.
- You'll go work for the competition.
- He or she will have to spend months looking for someone as good as you to replace you.
- He or she will then have to spend months working with someone new to finally get them to do your job just as good as you do it now.

Do you see where this is going?

Your boss doesn't have all the power. You do. And the best way to understand how you can use that power to stick it to your boss is to draw an analogy between your boss and a lobster.

As you may know, the way to cook a lobster or crab is to rub his head before you throw him live into a pot of boiling water. He will fall asleep and won't know what hit him. If you want to stick it to your boss, you have to think of him as a lobster or crab, and then rub his or her head, figuratively speaking, so he falls asleep under your spell.

And, figuratively speaking, here's how you cast that spell:

- Cheerfully work hard every day.
- Cheerfully work tirelessly every day.
- Cheerfully go above and beyond the call of duty every day.

And if you do this, your boss will soon stop worrying about you, stop worrying about all the things you are taking care of for him, and begin to count on you for

more and more as you free him up to do other things.

And BAM! It's happened! You've done such a good job of rubbing your boss the crab's head that, with respect to you, he has fallen asleep. This is important because now that you've carefully trained your boss to depend on you and take you for granted, you can lower the boom by starting to make demands for:

- More money
- More responsibility
- More vacation time
- More, more, more everything

And if you set things up right in advance, what choice is your boss going to have? Your boss will know that he can either give you everything you want or lose you and risk never being able to find someone as good as you, as dependable as you, as hardworking as you, ever again.

Congratulations! You just stuck it to the man!

ACKNOWLEDGMENTS

Writing your first book isn't an easy task. There were many agonizing days, wasted time, sleepless nights, and countless thoughts about how it should be written, structured, and presented. A book represents something unique about your life, how you live, and how you see the world. I wanted this book to be a conduit of my thoughts and a vessel to deliver them to my fellow human beings.

The journey was a challenging one. Fortunately, my dreams and desires have been supported and encouraged by hundreds of people all around the world. Directly and indirectly, I have turned to these people for knowledge, inspiration, and guidance. Without them, this book wouldn't be possible.

I believe it is important to always take inventory of the people in our lives. Success is not created alone or overnight. At many points in our lives (especially mine), someone has lent us a helping hand or given us an extra push. It is only appropriate—and necessary—to acknowledge some of these great people who've been a part of my life. I also dedicate this book to them as a small gesture of my appreciation.

My journey will always be guided by those who've given their time, love, energy, wisdom, and insight over the years. I am eternally grateful.

Peace and Love,

—Ronald

Helen Moore (*Mom*)

Skyhorse Staff

Grandma Tenisa Rudolph

Collie Cook, Jr., and Family

Danielle Baker

Christopher Baker

Andra Thompson

Rob and Kristie McNealy

Calvin and Dana Lotz

Timothy Miller and Family

Boz Scaggs

Donald J. Schneider

Patrick Manns

Larry and Rebecca Duke

Tommy Sims

The Hay Family

Austin Hill

Wendy Moten

Micah Baldwin

Brian Freeman and Family

Jeff Barr

Chris Brogan

Terry White

Earnest Shelvin

David Cohen

Uncle Tony Moore

Jeff Robinson (*HCA*)

Charlotte Davis

Ronald Lewis (*Dad*)

Aunt Sandy McCreary

Grandpa Robert Rudolph, Sr.

Morton Beard and Family

Herbert Baker, Jr.

Deborah Baker

Brad and Jeannine Crooks

Dave Taylor

Dr. Randy Pausch (*CMU*)

Michael McDonald and Family

William "Bill" H. Gates (*Microsoft*)

Adaeze McDaniel

Jerome Payne and Family

Craig Newmark

Nathan East

The Russell Family

Peter Schiff

Charles J. Orlando

Tara Anderson

Tom McCracken

Karen Brady

Liz Burr

Julie Byerlein

Bernie Chiaravalle

Aunt Sylvia Cross

Uncle Roosevelt Cross

David Young (*HCA*)

Allen Dietzel

Gregg and Jody Stebben

Grandma Louise Johnson

David Parham, Sr.

Uncle Rufus Moore

Herbert Baker, Sr.

Cassius Thompson

Stephen Sven Hultquist and Family

Kit Seeborg

Paul and Teresa Patterson

Kirk Whalum

Johnnie Bryan Hunt (*J.B. Hunt*)

Dr. Ron Paul

Jerry Payne and Family

Kim "Kem" Owens

Andrew Cook and Family

Matthew Matchovitz

Kenny Loggins

Jeremy Tanner

Ted Wahler

Growers Organic Crew

Arin Weibers

Lonnie Busby

Gary Campbell and Family

Stephen Clancy

Uncle James Moore

Michael Curcio (*HCA*)

Kristi Davidson

David Farber (*CMU*)

John Fischer

Lynne d Johnson

Tom Keller

Twitter.com community

Dawn Mikkelson

Mike Sippie

Noelle Stepherson

Brian Tsuchiya

Samantha Wender

Les Brown

Dave Webb

Amy Gahran

Chris Kauza

Darryl Kyles

Suzette L. McPherson

Jennifer Oikle, Ph.D.

Vincent Smith

Gina Stepherson

Dave Walls

Michael Hogan

Tom Cryer

Paul Swansen

Elizabeth Harms

Tom Keating

Ross MacLoed

Jim Van Meggelen

Kenneth J. Reed

Philipe Williams

Raymond Thomas and Family

Cynthia D. Webb

Kent Wien

Alex Jones

Linda Rutherford (*Southwest*)